Black Education in White America

SHUKDEB SEN PhD

NEWMAN SPRINGS PUBLISHING
320 Broad Street
Red Bank, NJ 07701

First originally published by Newman Springs Publishing 2018

ISBN 978-1-64096-383-2 (Paperback)
ISBN 978-1-64096-384-9 (Digital)

Printed in the United States of America

For my brother, Bhudeb Sen
(April 17, 1941–January 10, 1964)
You taught me how to dream the impossible dream,
Inspired me and showed me the beacon of hope in humanity.
I miss you, and I will love you always.

And to my wife, Dr. Sulakshana Sen
Your encouragement and sacrifice made it possible,
Without it, this book would never see the light.

CONTENTS

During the creation of the American Republic, two major institutions were born: slavery and poverty. Poor White class and African slaves were part of the domain of poverty and their main role was to provide labor and physical comfort for the upper-class White financier, nobility, merchants, plantation owners, and other elites. Two classes dominated the young republic—the haves and have-nots. As slavery and agricultural slave labor force exploded in Southern part of the Republic, a third tier of a class system embedded in America—where slaves were the mainstay.

Two hundred forty-one years have gone by but the institution of poverty is still growing steadily and over forty million people are under its grip. It is growing every day in America. The slavery has been abolished but the legacy of slavery is controlling the lives of African-Americans as a marginalized group. Dominant White culture always puts down African-American population as inferior, lazy, and anti-social elements, and carries a strong fear against these people.

As an educator, the author had the privilege to teach thousands of African-Americans, Africans, and other racial groups in post-secondary educational institutions. Through the years, one fact has become a constant where numerous African-American students show a deficit in academic preparedness and performance. The majority of the Black students born in Africa and the Caribbean showed excellent performance in all fields of studies and secured high levels of accomplishment. It was obvious that Black race has nothing to do with poor academic performance. A large number of African-Americans are somehow prone to nonperformance in academic sphere. To find the answer for this academic question, why do African-American students perform poorly in academia, this book was born. Extensive scientific literature research revealed that the legacy of slavery was responsible for the development of destructive toxic stress and trauma experiences, which caused extensive damage via epigenetic modification of DNA and histone proteins. This has caused various psychosocial, neurobiological abnormalities and diseases among millions of African-American people in America for centuries.

Slavery was common in almost all cultures in the world. Most cultures absorbed the institution of slavery and slaves into the main social milieu became a part of the society through social acceptance. But the American institution of slavery kept a policy of segregation and non-acceptance and maintained a distance from African-Americans. Descendants of slaves were never allowed to be absorbed in the society, and always segregated policies prevailed. Cultural amalgamation and assimilation was never attempted by the White majority. For this reason, African-Americans as a group live in a quasi-segregated existence in America. The Native Americans lived in isolation from mainstream America because they were literally eliminated through massive genocide, intentionally executed by the Whites. Those who survived the genocide and their descendants were kept in isolation in Indian reservations, where utter poverty, disease, and social decimation slowly stole their lives.

African-Americans suffered untold inhuman torture such as rape, lynching, and treatment as nonhuman subjects below even cattle and other livestock during slavery and beyond. All these experiences led African-Americans a group of humans who lost all hope and aspirations. Hopelessness consumed their desire to fight against all negative experiences, and to them life as a meaningless existence.

During the writing of this book, the author came across the influence of racism, caste systems, academic and intellectual slavery that subsumed the operation and process of post-secondary education in America. American education has been following a dichotomous path so that it can keep segregation in an educational enterprise alive as long as possible. The dominant Whites felt it necessary to maintain the practice of educational segregation so that they can retain the power and privileges. As time approaches the demographic shift where whites will be a minority group in 2050, the dominant

White feel their power of controlling all privileges such as education, finance, job opportunities, and running this country slowly slipping away. They fear losing their power and control over people might bring further racial tension/discord/disturbance in America down the road.

America needs to embrace the true meaning of education where freedom is the essence. To achieve this, the educational system must be transparent and discard the policy of segregation. Universal educational opportunities must be provided to every person living in this country. In the international arena, American education is falling behind. If this nation wants to maintain its leadership position, it must act now. Education is the force that can eliminate poverty, raise living standards, reduce diseases and other maladies, create cohesiveness, and instill hope and happiness to its people. Negative experiences like trauma and toxic stress caused epigenetic modification in DNA and histone proteins, which inflicted serious neurobiological changes among African-Americans and was passed on from one generation to the next. It is possible that positive, hopeful, and enlightenment via educational inclusiveness can create higher achievements that can propel epigenetic modification of DNA into reversing the ill effects and/or detrimental neurobiological changes.

Education brings hope and it can liberate people from racism and in group-outgroup divisiveness. America needs educational reform and openness. Education is the birthright for humanity and it is the force that can guide the humanity to freedom where human minds can fly from one corner to the other without any bondage and oppressions. This book, *Black Education in White America*, attempts to open the window of American education in general, and in particular, the African-American education in the US.

CHAPTER 1

A Nation at Risk

"A Nation at Risk" was the title of the report President Reagan presented to the public on April 26, 1983, at the White House about the state of education in the United States of America. A panel of experts representing the National Commission on Excellence in Education wrote this report at the request of the education secretary Terrell Bell. It stated that "if an unfriendly foreign power had attempted to impose on America the mediocre educational performance that exists today, we might well have viewed it as an act of war."

This report continued to emphasize that "the educational foundations of our society are being eroded by a rising tide of mediocrity that threatens our future as a nation and a people" (National Commission on Excellence in Education, 1983).

This warning regarding deterioration of education in America was based on the indicators of the risk such as international comparisons of student achievement. Millions of adults and about 13 percent of all seventeen -year-olds are illiterate because of poor reading, writing, and comprehension skills. A continuous decline in the College Board's Scholastic Aptitude Tests (SAT) among our high school students shows that our educational system is in crisis.

Education Secretary Bell quoted from the report that, "Our society and its educational institutions seem to have lost sight of the basic purposes of schooling, and of the high expectations and disciplined effort needed to attain them." He suggested to, "Generate reform our educational system in fundamental ways and to renew the nation's commitment to schools and colleges of high quality throughout the length and breadth of our land."

This report stated that twenty-three million American adults are illiterate, whereas about 13 percent of all seventeen-year-olds and 40 percent minority youths are illiterate. The College Board's Scholastic aptitude tests (SAT) showed a continuous decline from 1963 to 1980. The average verbal score fell fifty points, whereas, in mathematics the average dropped forty points. Many seventeen-year-olds lack higher-order intellectual skills and 40 percent cannot derive conclusions from facts (United States National Commission on Excellence 1983). Science achievement scores of seventeen-year-olds declined in private and public four-year colleges. Similarly, the 72 percent increase in remedial mathematics courses in colleges shows a serious problem involving mathematical thinking and computing skills among students. This deficiency led military leaders to pronounce that recent recruits cannot read and understand safety manual operating modern military hardware.

Decline in education can jeopardize our preeminence in agriculture, commerce, industry, medicine, science, and technological innovation in the global arena because education is the driving force for the progress, freedom, enlightenment, and civility in mankind.

State of Education in America

Thirty-three years later American education is still at risk. Performance of fifteen-year-old American students on the Program for International Student Assessment (PISA) is not encouraging. In 2012 average scores in mathematics literacy ranged from 368 to 613. The US average mathematics score was 481, which is lower than the average for all Organization for Economic Co-operation and Development (OECD) countries (494), and twenty-nine countries scored higher than US average score (OECD, Education GPS). In science, literacy test average scores ranged from 373 to 580. The US average science score was 497, which was very similar to OECD average score (501). Twenty-two countries had higher average scores in science than the US.

High levels of proficiency in science and mathematics are the most essential ingredients for driving our technological advancement, which provide intellectual products that maintains our superiority in medicine, economics, and sciences over other nations. In a global economy and technological competition, we must maintain our preeminence, and to sustain it we have to have our workforce trained and proficient in mathematics and science.

Thirty years have passed since President Reagan's announcement in 1983 regarding "A Nation at Risk." A new report came out from the Education Secretary Arne Duncan's office in 2013 where he raised a new alarm that said, "Threat of educational stagnation and complacency" is engulfing the nation (Duncan 2013).

Education Secretary Duncan's report was based on the results from the Program for International Students Assessment (PISA). The assessment provides a comparative analysis of US performance of fifteen-year-olds in high school around the globe. PISA focuses on the core school subjects in reading, mathematics, and science. The assessment requires students to gain the knowledge and skills and examine how well students can use the knowledge to solve problems familiar and unfamiliar ones through innovation and higher order thinking processes.

Secretary Duncan stated that "in a knowledge-based global economy where education is more important than ever before, both to the individual success and collective prosperity, our students are losing ground. We're running in place, as other high-performing countries start to lap us. Fifteen-year-olds in the US today are average in science and reading literacy, and below average in mathematics, compared to where their counterparts are in OECD countries" (Duncan 2013).

PISA academic performance examination used by sixty-two education systems in both 2009 and 2012, US students ranked twenty-fourth in 2009 and twenty-ninth in 2012 in mathematics according to the OECD, whereas, in science US ranked nineteenth in 2009 and dropped to twenty-second in 2012; US ranking in reading dropped tenth to twentieth in 2012, (Duncan 2013).

Hanusek et al., (2014) used a crosswalk studies between the National Assessment of Educational Progress (NAEP) and PISA tests by "identifying levels of performance on PISA that yield equivalent proportions of US students that meet the NAEP proficiency and advanced standards," assuming that all eighth graders "who pass the NAEP proficiency bar" in mathematics would also "pass a similar threshold on the PISA test next year" (Hanusek et al. 2014).

The result of the study revealed that when viewed from a global perspective, US schools do a poor job in teaching students from better educated families and students from less well-educated families. Overall, the US proficiency rate in math is 35 percent, which places US at twenty-seventh among thirty-four OECD countries (Hanusek et al. 2014).

The analysis shows a wide range of proficiency rate across states when parental education levels are included. Students from the household of high levels of parental education have high proficiency in math. For example, in Massachusetts students from educated families show 62 percent proficiency in math, which would rank the state just behind Germany and Switzerland, two of the top five OECD countries. States like Vermont, Minnesota, Colorado, New Jersey, and Montana have math proficiency rates 58 to 59 percent among students from educated families. This will translate with OECD countries that rank among top thirteen in the PISA test. States like California (43%), New York (40%), and Florida (38%) would assume on OECD ranking 30, 31, and 32 positions (Hanusek et al., 2014). Students from families with low parental educational levels show highest proficiency level in Texas (28%) and lowest in California (8%), Virginia (6%), and Utah (5%). From this, the authors concluded that "educational shortcomings in the United States spread well beyond the corridors of inner-city or the confines of low-income neighborhoods where many parents lack a high school diploma . . . the overall picture is distressing to those concerned about the well-being of the United States in the 21st century" (Hanusek et al. 2014).

Many scholars believe PISA test scores are flawed and based on a "profound conceptual error" (Stewart, 2013). They believe scores are incorrect and ranking for US is not accurate. Carnoy and Rothstein (2013) did an extensive analysis of the PISA scores for the year 2009 where American students ranked fourteenth in reading and twenty-fifth in mathematics. They found that the rankings are not accurate because they have sampling error and over-representation of most disadvantaged school test takers in the pool of students. They observed that in every country students at the bottom of the social class distribution performed worse than students who were higher in the distribution. In the US we have a high social class inequality than any other comparable countries in the world; we have a very large number of students taking the test who were ill-prepared. This has been pronounced in the PISA 2009 test. A severe sampling error occurred during the PISA test where students from the most disadvantaged schools were over-represented in the overall US test takers source. These errors caused depressed test scores.

Their analysis showed that for US adolescents with similar social class distribution such as France, Germany, and United Kingdom, then the average reading scores for US will be higher and average math scores for US will be same average as similar post industrial countries. Thus, re-estimated analysis would improve US ranking to sixth (6th) in reading and thirteenth (13th) in mathematics (Carnoy and Rothstein 2013).

The most recent PISA (2015) examination revealed that US fifteen-year-olds scores declined further in the ranking in science, reading, and mathematics from 2009 to 2015 as shown in Table 1.

Table 1. Average scores and rank of fifteen-year-old students from US on PISA tests in science, reading, and mathematics: 2000, 2003, 2006, 2009, 2012, and 2015.[1]

Year	2000	2003	2006	2009	2012	2015
Subject	Av. Score/ Rank	Av. Score/ Rank	Av. Score/ Rank	Av. Score/ Rank	Av. Score/ Rank	Av. Score/ Rank
Science Literacy	X X	X X	489 17	502 19	497 22	496 19
Mathematics Literacy	X X	483 X	474 32	487 24	481 29	470 37
Reading Literacy	504 X	495 X	X X	500 10	498 20	497 15

The analysis of composite scores in science, math, and reading from the year 2000 to 2015 showed our fifteen-year-old performing poorly when compared with the other countries. Even when we recalculate the errors built in the PISA evaluative process, it is crystal clear that our students are not moving forward to gain various skills in critical thinking, problem solving, and innovative thinking essential to compete globally.

The SAT scores also show a steady decline in reading, mathematics and writing for the college-bound high school seniors (Table 2).

---

[1] This table represents a modified Table 4 in Performance of US fifteen-year-old students in Science, Mathematics, and Reading Literacy in an International context (NCES 2017-048). Data source: Organization for Economic Cooperation and Development (OECD), Program for International Student Assessment (PISA), 2000, 2003, 2006, 2009, 2012, and 2015. Also, selected findings from PISA-2012, 2015. Retrieved from https://nces.ed.gov/surveys/pisa/pisa2015/pisa2015highlights_1.asp

Table 2. SAT mean scores of college bound seniors: Selected years 2000-01 through 2014-15 (Re-centered Scale)[2]

School Year	Critical Reading Scores	Mathematics Scores	Writing Scores
2001–02	504	516	-
2002–03	507	519	-
2003–04	508	518	-
2004–05	508	520	-
2005–06	503	518	497
2006–07	502	515	494
2007–08	502	515	494
2008–09	501	515	493
2009–10	501	516	492
2010–11	497	514	489
2011–12	496	514	488
2012–13	496	514	488
2013–14	497	513	487
2014–15	495	511	484

This problem is a pernicious drainage of American intellect should be addressed. It is easy to blame the minority population for the decline in the test scores, but one of the main reasons for this negativity is because of social class inequality that resulted in poverty, which is rotting the core of American populace through toxic stress. These toxic stresses generated by the poverty must be stopped; otherwise, we will see a steady decline in not only academic sectors but also every faces of economic, social, cultural aspects of this great country of ours. It is difficult to understand why the US spends trillions of dollars on defense spending for the "perceived fear/threat from foreign countries" when we know that there is no country on the earth capable of doing any harm to the US, but the US is not willing to take measures that would eliminate poverty and create a

---

[2] U.S. Department of Education, National Center for Education Statistics. 2016. Digest of Education Statistics, 2015 (NCES 2016-014), Table 226.10 Retrieved August 30, 2017 from: https://nces.ed.gov/fastfacts/display.asp?id=171.

new value system for meaningful education that would uplift citizens in a higher plane toward educational fulfillment and raise the quality of living standards in an open, fair, and just democratic society.

CHAPTER 2

What Is Education?

To define the term *education*, we will use ideas from some distinguished scholars so we can have a better understanding of the meaning of education and develop an appreciation for it. Philip Jackson (2012; 95) stated that "education is a facilitated process of cultural transmission whose explicit goal is to effect an enduring change for the better in the character and psychological well-being (the personhood) of its recipients and, by indirection, in their broader social environment, which extends to the world at-large."

According to Jackson (2012; 95) the central mission of education has five types of truths: factual, systemic, instrumental, moral, and subjective truths.

1. Factual truths – one should gather factual information from all sources.
2. Systemic truths – concepts or ideas are held together through logical deductive reasoning and they are capable of expansion if nurtured, or they can fade away if they are not cultivated rationally.
3. Instrumental truths – they are the guiding light or pathways that tell us how things can work.
4. Moral truths – these groups are the guiding principles for all of us to lead our lives in a civil and righteous way among people in the community.
5. Subjective truths – the ideas how an individual perceives him or herself within the society. The interplay of self-per-

ception and the influence of transmitted ideas from other individuals are very important for the complete assimilation that becomes a permanent component of self-realization.

Beside these five truths, three types of thought processes are intertwined in the essence of education according to Jackson (2012). One of the main tasks of education is to channel the human thought in a proper focus and direction, as the thought has a tendency to drift from one direction to another. Often, it shifts to a different dimension where there is no connection (Jackson, 2012). He described thoughts follow three major tracks such as horizontally, vertically, or elliptically. Horizontal thought represents a growth of knowledge, vertical thought seeks the finality or closure of the subject, and elliptical thought exerts positive assertion on the validity of the subject.

Sir Richard Livingstone (1953) stated that education teaches us how to express ourselves to others, think clearly and logically, develop or exercise the inherent sensibilities that comes from the inside, and show willingness to correct self-knowledge when it is necessary. He emphasized the idea of "first rate," where he stated "education must be the midwife—the metaphor suggests one of the most fruitful and fundamental conceptions in that field—and bring to birth this philosophy of the first rate, which is so fruitful and which no human being would disown. First-rate can only be recognized by seeing it and can only be taught by looking at it."

One of the most influential philosophers and educators, John Dewey, proposed that education must be based on experience, freedom, democracy, and scientific methods. Human experiences are the driving force for the attainment of knowledge that is a cornerstone of education.

Dewey (1938; 8) believed experience play an important role in education. According to him there is an "organic connection between education and personal experience."

He emphasized that "problems are the stimulus to thinking" because "the problem grows out of the conditions of the experience being had in the present and that it is within the range of the capacity of students. It arouses in the learner and active quest for information and for production of new ideas. The new facts and new ideas thus obtained become the ground for further experiences in which new problems me presented" (Dewey; 1938, 34).

He also realized that all experiences are not educational. Some experiences "may be immediately enjoyable and yet promote the formation of a slack and careless attitude; this attitude then operates to modify the quality of subsequent experiences to prevent a person from getting out of them what they have to give." This can lead to disconnect and the "consequence of formation of such habits is an inability to control future experiences" (Dewey; 1938, 8–9).

Dewey's analysis of habits plays a major role in the process of education. Habits are usually thought of as mental makeup or a usual manner of a behavior pattern that influences attitude whether it is "emotional or intellectual," and it covers "our basic sensitivities and ways of meeting and responding to all conditions which we meet in living." This idea delineates that "the principle of continuity of experience means that every experience both takes up something from those which have gone before and modifies in some way the quality of those which came after" (13).

Dewey emphasized the importance of freedom in the process of education because he believed "freedom is power: power to frame purposes, to judge wisely, to evaluate desires by the consequences which will result from acting upon them" (27). He noted that human desire and impulses are connected to the ideas of education. Impulses can compromise or derail the formation of intelligent judgment, which is detrimental to intellectual growth. Dewey declared that the "ideal aim of education is a creation of power of self-control" (28).

Dewey (1938) believed education should follow scientific method which will allow an individual to gain knowledge through meaningful positive experiences that will be open for correction/ alteration if needed, and these experiences will modify the attitude, habits, and skill set of that individual. He was a champion of democratic idealism and he incorporated ideals of democracy in developing his scaffolding for education. He believed in a democratic society. A better quality of human experiences can be experienced and these experiences can be enjoyed fully, which will translate into a better assimilation of knowledge and educational fulfillment.

According to Smith (2015) education is "the wise, hopeful and respectful cultivation of learning undertaken in the belief that all should have the chance to share in life." Learning is a process and an outcome. It should be deliberate and hopeful so that people can set out to make happen in the belief that people can "be more" informed, respectful, and wise, so that this process can and should invite the truth and anticipate possibility. It must be grounded in the idea and belief that all should flourish and shares achievement that uplift their existence or live as best as possible in a peaceful society.

Hope is an essential attribute in the process of learning if the inherent energy within a human being which drives the engine of doing something worth doing. If this energy is missing then the person will experience a void that will douse the bright flames of the desire/quest of learning. Hope is linked with another powerful attribute of living that is self-belief (Warnock; 1986, 182).

Hope has been engraved in more religious tones, but it is a force that is enveloped in human cognitive experience guided by neuro-physiological expression. According to MacQuarrie (1978), "Hope carries in itself a definite way to understanding both ourselves and the environing processes within which human life has its setting" (11).

Education helps us to make sense of things and allow us to work to find the meaning and for the solution that would garner better outcome and positive changes. Education must hold truth at a higher plane. Searching for the truth is the driving force of gathering knowledge that we can substantiate through rigorous analysis, and have the courage to reject the unfounded, non-applicable knowledge (Smith 2015).

Education is a multifaceted concept that encompasses many types of ideas. The meaning of education varies based on the person trying to understand this complex process involving cognitive, behavioral, psychological, social, innovative, and human qualities. To summarize what education is we can say: education is a lifelong process where a person gains knowledge, skills, habits, and social consciousness through various mediums of communication, instruction, and share formal and/or informal settings that will guide the person throughout his/her life the pathway of meaningful existence in a free, civil, and democratic society.

Education teaches us how to lead a meaningful existence in a civil, free, and democratic society. It will be the leading force that can transform and elevate a person into a higher plane where that individual can contribute to uplift the society, if proper conditions are available and nurtured.

What is learning?

Oxford Dictionary defines learning as "the acquisition of knowledge or skills through study, experience or being taught."

Dewey emphasized that the process of learning must depend on the continuous progressive march toward growth through "reconstruction or reorganization of experience, which adds to the meaning of experience, and which increases the ability to direct the course of subsequent experiences" (Dewey; 1916, 76).

Learning is an active part of the educational process where pupils gain knowledge via two contrasting approaches: "Having" and "Being" modes (Fromm 1979). Having mode focuses on possessing or owning something. In educational learning platform, possessing knowledge or whatever learned became a personal acquisition that is carefully cultivated or stored in the memory. These learned material or facts are tangible but do not have the power of creating new knowledge (Fromm 1979). In contrast, "Being," according to Fromm (1979), is connected with shared experiences and productive activities that can lead to create new knowledge, high levels of creativity, and innovative accomplishment.

In the twenty-first century the skill sets for educated individual are different from the skill sets of the twentieth century. A major and dramatic shift of the skill sets uses the "adaptive expertise" where a greater cognitive ability as well as capacity are necessary ingredients for maintaining the competitive edge (Dumont et al., 2010). Adaptive expertise is the ability to apply learned knowledge to various situations through skillful, imaginative, and creative ways that bring greater rewards and successful culmination of the task or endeavor. This ability not only exceeds the mastery of the discipline but also exhibits a strong desire to change, adapt, and expand the capabilities of the gained expertise so that learning can continue throughout the life (Dumont et al., 2010).

The demand for higher-order skills has been exploding in all facets of work environment and in the society. Individuals must have the following skills to be considered educated in the twenty-first century (Dumont et al., 2010):

1. Ability to generate, process, and sort complex information.
2. Ability to think critically and analyze the information in a systematic and effective way.
3. Ability to make decisions based on the available information through a process of inductive reasoning.
4. Ability to ask questions that are based on higher order of intellectual maturity and meaningful for everyone.
5. Ability to be creative and desire innovative ideas.
6. Ability to solve real-world problems and be a good team player with excellent communication skills.

Lifelong learning habits are based on the development of attitudes that gain value, desire, skills, and knowledge throughout the pre- and post-secondary educational experiences and nourish the aptitude that laid the foundation for lifelong and self-directed learning.

The technological innovations, knowledge economies, and global competition among nations are driving the demand for people with a higher level of cognitive expertise. Without the expertise, individuals cannot compete, and will be outsiders and dispensable.

Transmission of education

Transmission of education follows two major tracks. The traditional formal transmission (Formalists) is where learners are treated as "objects" and needed to be "molded." Formalists believe education is about passing information, because human civilization and cultural practices carry a tremendous amount of information that enlightened the human history filled with ideas and wisdom, and must pass down to the next generation. Here the emphasis is on transmission. In contrast, the progressives believe the learners have the natural curiosity of learning things around them, and they want to immerse through their own initiative in the knowledge, ideas, beliefs, culture, vision, and extracted the truth from within. This will create and expand new sets of knowledge or new learning experiences that would accentuate their learning abilities (Thomas 2013).

Why education is important

Education is the driving force for the emancipation of the mind. It brings hope and aspiration to life and allows an individual to dream for a better, prosperous, and meaningful life. It provides the real meaning of living and leads us to a path where wisdom guides us to look for answers that would be just, equitable, and fair for all. It is a birthright for all individuals and must be available to everybody with no prejudice, disparity, segregation, and bondage (Satyarthi 2014).

It has the power to eliminate poverty, hunger, disease, and it can stimulate the economic progress, prosperity, and living standard for all people. It can guide us in a path where peace and tolerance among various groups of people can flourish. Education is the power and a beacon of hope for mankind.

CHAPTER 3

State of Education in Black America

Education in America since the slavery to present times follows a distinct dichotomy based on denial or segregation. During British colonial America and the Revolutionary War, the slaves were denied rudiments of education as they were treated as a laborer whose main job was to provide services that would support the agro-economic machine for the planters and the elite class. Education was meaningless for these poor classes of people and never supported by the owners.

During the time of slavery, the Southern States slaves were forcefully denied the elements of education because whites feared it would elevate the slaves to a level where they might ask for some equality and rudiments of freedom. The planters and settlers suppressed the slaves' desire to even touch a book or learn how to read and write. The brutality and oppressive instruments were used to suppress the slaves so that these people would be illiterate and ignorant about their basic civil rights to express their sufferings and inhumane treatment to others.

After the end of Civil War, the creation of Freedmen's Bureau started a new era where the education was supported by the government and hundreds of primary, secondary, and post-secondary educational facilities were established so that millions of ex-slaves and poor Whites can break their shackles of illiteracy and ignorance, and become emancipated individuals. Ex-slaves exerted their power by virtue of their knowledge that their labor power was the driving force of the Southern agricultural machine that brought prosperity to their ex-masters and plantation owners prior to the Civil War and in the post-Civil War. Their labor power can restore the Southern agriculture and its prosperity together again. The ex-slaves demanded a better living wages and educational opportunities (Anderson 1988).

The Freedmen's Bureau supported the ex-slaves and responsible to include educational clauses in the labor contract. This help from the Freedmen's organization enhanced the ex-slaves' determination to get an education. Some Southern planters supported schooling for ex-slaves because they realized that by doing so it would stabilize the supply of laborers for their plantation and bring prosperity for them. For this reason, some planters even shielded Freedmen's schools from harassment by White supremacist groups (Anderson 1988).

The majority of White planters and poor Whites were against the ex-slaves' pursuit of universal schooling, and they believe that Blacks should not be educated at all. They were fearful about the determination and excellence in academic performance of ex-slaves, because they knew they could not compete with the people they had abused physically and mentally for centuries past.

Education provided the desire for self-determination responsible for achieving emancipation and economic stability. Booker T. Washington knew of these ideological strategies. He fought to establish them so that his people could achieve emancipation and economic stability by using the power of education. His farsightedness and genius used this ideology to prevent supremacist interference to his educational strategy and thwarted the attacks from the Ku Klux Klan and other supremacist demagogues.

The hope of all Blacks rested on the premise of getting literacy and formalized education that would allow them to be free, and open the window of opportunity, economic empowerment, and the quest for equality. Education is the power for the past, present, and the future. The dream to achieve liberation was through gaining an education. Schooling was an essential tool to facilitate the desire of "self-determination and the development of a vision outside the parameters of the White supremacist, missionaries, philanthropists, and capitalist of that time" (Bradley 2010).

Ex-slaves demanded access to schooling after the Civil War because they realized that their hope for liberation from the current conditions could only be achieved through education. Educated masses can provide the fuel that can propel the desire of freedmen among all people whose minds and body were shackled by the oppressor's grip through tyranny and brainwashed ideology of inferiority and illiteracy. Enslaved Blacks, through their sweat and blood, created a prosperous country from the forced labor extracted by the oppressor White's institutionalized slavery.

Some progress was made throughout the US by the ex-slaves in getting an education during the Reconstruction era but White legislators of the former Confederate States passed the "Black Codes" that created various obstacles for the ex-slaves to receive an education and exercise their civil rights. This caused severe disruption in the educational process. When the Reconstruction ended in 1877 via the Compromise of 1877, the educational opportunity for Blacks and poor Whites ended. The Southern ex-Confederate States wanted ex-slaves to return to de facto slavery. Southern Democrats gave away the presidency during the most disputed presidential election in 1876 to the Republican Rutherford B. Hayes with the understanding that the US military personnel should leave Southern States and end the Reconstruction era. As soon as Republican Hayes became the nineteenth president, he signed the documents into law.

The end of Reconstruction brought back Southern States to power where ex-Confederates took control of the government and created numerous new laws known as "Jim Crow" laws that encouraged the White supremacist ideology and a segregated existence. In 1881 the state of Tennessee passed the first segregation law in railroads, which acted like a cancer that spread with no control in the life of all inhabitants in the state, in the affairs of education, which led to educational segregation. Similar laws were implemented throughout all Southern States.

Segregation cemented itself in all matters in 1896, when the Supreme Court of the US in the *Plessy v. Ferguson* case ruled that racial segregation is constitutional, and it etched in the educational psyche of America. Everything must be segregated, barring African-

Americans from equal access to public facilities. The mantra of "separate but equal" was never properly addressed, because segregated education between Whites and Blacks were strictly adhered but never the "equal" part of the law was followed. The word *equal* never existed in the minds of White Southerners. Black education suffered due to lack of funding, poor resources, non-existing infrastructural support, no access to better teachers and other necessary physical facilities, and manpower issues. The segregated education stifled the progress of African-Americans and retarded the creativity, innovation, and intellectual expression. (History.com; n.d.)

In 1954, after fifty-eight years of segregated institutional bondage was broken wide open by the US Supreme Court in the *Brown v. Board of Education* case. They ruled that segregation is unconstitutional and must be dismantled forever. Segregation is illegal in America, but the spirit of segregation is flourishing everywhere in America, particularly in the sectors of an academic environment. Academic racial separation between Blacks and Whites is common in our lives today. Now we have a different level of educational segregation based on poverty, educational, economical, academic attainment and achievement gaps. There is a significant academic achievement gap between White and Black students (Table 1).

Table 1. PISA 2012 ranking of American students by race[3]

Country/Economy	Reading	Science	Mathematics	Mean
OECD	496	501	494	497
Asian Americans	550	546	549	548
White Americans	519	528	506	518
Multi-racial Americans	517	511	492	507
USA (Composite)	498	497	481	492
Hispanic Americans	478	462	455	465
African Americans	443	439	421	434

---

[3] Table 1 is constructed from the PISA posting of Steve Sailer based on Federal NCES data From PISA 2012 test results. Retrieved from: isteve.blogspot. com/2013/12/overall-pisa-ranking-include-america.html

Tables 2, 3, and 4 describe the SAT mean scores of college-bound seniors by race/ethnicity for Critical Reading, Mathematics, and Writing.

Table 2. SAT Mean scores for Critical Reading of college-bound seniors by race/ethnicity: Selected years, 2005–06 through 2014–15[4]

SAT Critical Reading	2005–06	2006–07	2007–08	2008–09	2009–10	2010–11	2011–12	2012–13	2013–14	2014–15
White	527	527	528	528	528	528	527	527	529	529
Black	434	433	430	429	429	428	428	431	431	431
Hispanic	458	459	455	455	454	451	447	450	451	449
Asian	510	514	513	516	519	517	518	521	523	525

Table 3. SAT Mean scores for Mathematics of college-bound seniors by race/ethnicity: Selected years, 2005–06 through 2014–15[5]

SAT Mathematics	2005–06	2006–07	2007–08	2008–09	2009–10	2010–11	2011–12	2012–13	2013–14	2014–15
White	536	534	537	536	536	535	536	534	534	534
Black	429	429	426	426	428	427	428	429	429	428
Hispanic	463	463	461	461	462	462	461	461	459	457
Asian	578	578	581	587	591	595	595	597	598	598

---

[4] Data from Table 226.10, U.S. Department of Education, National Center for Education Statistics (2016). Digest of Education Statistics, 2015 (NCES 2016-014). Retrieved from: https://nces.ed.gov/fastfacts/display.asp?id=171

[5] Data from Table 226.10, U.S. Department of Education, National Center for Education Statistics (2016). Digest of Education Statistics, 2015 (NCES 2016-014). Retrieved from: https://nces.ed.gov/fastfacts/display.asp?id=171

Table 4. SAT Mean scores for Writing of college-bound seniors by race/ethnicity: Selected years, 2005–06 through 2014–15[6]

SAT Writing	2005–06	2006–07	2007–08	2008–09	2009–10	2010–11	2011–12	2012–13	2013–14	2014–15
White	519	518	518	517	516	516	515	515	513	513
Black	428	425	424	421	420	417	417	418	418	418
Hispanic	450	450	448	448	447	444	442	443	443	439
Asian	512	513	516	520	526	528	528	527	530	531

Reardon (2015) studied the effects of segregation on educational inequality and asked questions, "Does segregation exacerbate racial educational inequality? Or the association of racial segregation with unequal schooling or neighborhood conditions?" The Supreme Court ruled in *Brown v. Board of Education* that "separate educational facilities are inherently unequal," and argued that legally sanctioned segregation on the basis of race damaged psychologically the mind, spirit, and aspiration of Black children, which cannot be repaired by adjusting the school facilities and resources. The "act of legal exclusion" was responsible for the inequality and violated the Fourteenth Amendment.

Coleman et al. (1966) wrote, "The higher achievement of all racial and ethnic groups in schools with great proportions of White students is largely, perhaps wholly related to effects associated with a student body's educational background and aspirations" (307). Differences in socioeconomic composition of schools (high poverty/ low poverty) dictate the achievement gaps among Black and White students.

Reardon's research analyzed sixteen distinct measures of segregation. These measures determined the most probable factors responsible for the academic achievement gap between White and Black students. He found that "the disparity in average school poverty rates

---

[6] Data from Table 226.10, U.S. Department of Education, National Center for Education Statistics (2016). Digest of Education Statistics, 2015 (NCES 2016-014). Retrieved from: https://nces.ed.gov/fastfacts/display.asp?id=171

between White and Black students' schools is the single most powerful correlate of achievement gaps" (Reardon 2015). The simple translation of this finding revealed that high poverty schools are much less effective than low poverty schools. Black students are receiving poor educational experiences because of a segregated school system.

The US Government Accountability Office (GAO) reported that from 2000–2001 to the 2013–2014 school year K–12 public schools in a high poverty area catering African-American and Hispanic students grew from 7,009 schools to 15,089 schools, and the percentage of all schools with so-called racial or socioeconomic isolation grew from 9 percent to 16 percent. These "isolated schools" had over 75 percent or more students representing same race or class (Toppo 2016).

US representative John Conyers, a Democrat, after reading the GAO study report said, "It confirms what long has been feared and proves that current barriers against educational inequality are eerily similar to those fought during the Civil Rights movement. There simply can be no excuse for allowing educational apartheid in the 21st century." US education Secretary John King commented "Six decades after Brown v. Board, we have failed to close opportunity and achievement gaps for our African-American and Latino students at every level of education. And far too many schools, we continue to offer them less—less access to the best teachers and most challenging courses, less access to the services and support that affluent students often take for granted, and less access to what it takes to succeed academically."

Educational disparity, segregated educational policies dictated by the economic conditions, achievement gap, and a touch of racial prejudice is the state of education in the African-American's America.

CHAPTER 4

Race and Racism

The word *race* according to Dictionary.com Unabridged is defined as "an arbitrary classification of modern humans, sometimes, especially formerly, based on any or a combination of various physical characteristics, as skin color, facial form, or eye shape, and now frequently based on such genetic markers as blood groups" (Dictionary. com). This definition, however, cannot convey the impact of this simple word on its association to people all over the world, regarding ethnicity, slavery, culture, oppression, subjugation, hatred, extermination, and persecution. This word evokes a psychological response to people. To understand this, one has to delve himself into the history, scientific, social, anthropological, and cultural aspects, so that the individual can arrive to a meaningful outcome. Between the sixteenth and eighteenth centuries, the word *race* was a folk idea in English language and was used to express type, kind, breed, and species (Allen 1994, Smedley 1999a).

However, during the Revolutionary era, the word *race* gained a new meaning where emphasis was on the social aspect of skin color classified as White, Indians, and Blacks (Allen 1994, 1997; Smedley 1999 b). The transformation of the word *race* into a major social construct of race was necessary to justify the era of colonialism and subjugation of people through conquest. A new ideology based on human difference such as skin color has to be established so that the subjugated race can be used as slaves (Allen 1994; Fredrickson 1988, 2002; Morgan 1975; Smedley 1999b).

Imposition of slavery on people of color by the superior enlightened White Christians needed a moral sanction that if the subjects are non-human being or savages, then it will be an acceptable practice to follow (Smedley and Smedley 2005; Haller 1971).

Audrey Smedley (1999b) summarized the diagnostic social characteristics of race used in North America as follows:

1. Physical characteristics such as skin color, hair texture, eye shape, and other facial features were used as markers for racial groups.
2. Belief that racial groups are unequal and Africans belong to lowest rank or level.
3. Belief that physical features are innate and heritable.
4. Differences among races are unchangeable.

The scientific analyses of the concept of race reveal the following facts as described by Mukhopadhyay et al. (2014).

1. Visible phenotypical variation skin color, hair texture, and facial features cannot be used to classify people into different racial categories.
2. Environmental factors control the color of skin in people with different shades of pigmentation is not a valid argument to categorize people into different races.
3. Lewontin (1972) demonstrated that "based on randomly chosen genetic differences, human races and populations are similar to each other, with the largest part by far of human variation being accounted for by the differences between individuals" (397). This means that there is more diversity within the same group of people than between other groups belong to different regions.
4. Gene frequency analysis of blood system groups and protein obtained from aboriginal populations from all parts of the world revealed that all modern humans are members of one species, *Homo sapiens*, which originated in Africa (Cavalli-Sforza 2000).

Mitochondrial DNA analysis of samples from all over Europe showed that most native Europeans connected to maternal ancestor who came from Africa (Sykes 2001). All humans living today belong to the same biological species *Homo sapiens*, originated from Africa, eons ago. For this reason, it is safe to conclude that the concept of "race" has no biological or evolutionary basis and no meaningful credence to it. It is, however, a social construct manufactured to justify the abuse and oppression of people by the dominant groups for their own economic benefit and maintain cultural dominance over the subordinate groups.

In this context it will be appropriate to state what Du Bois thought of the concept of race as follows, "I think it was in Africa that I came more clearly see the close connection between race and wealth. The fact that even in the minds of the most dogmatic supporters of race theories and believers in the inferiority of colored folks to white, there was a conscious or unconscious determination to increase their incomes by taking full advantage of this belief. And then gradually these thought was metamorphosed into a realization that the income-bearing value of race prejudice was the cause and not the result of theories of race inferiority; that particularly in the United States the income of the Cotton Kingdom based on black slavery caused the passionate belief in Negro inferiority and the determination to enforce it even by arms" (Du Bois; 2007, 65).

All living systems discriminate.

All living systems have developed an ability to discriminate or have "preference" that allows them to face challenges and survive in various environmental conditions that may not be conducive for living. This ability is one of the most fundamental behavioral "preferences" all living organisms possess that ensures their survival (Stanley et al. 2003). Any organism unable to adjust, adapt, and change would be eliminated from this world.

Primitive human ancestors experienced constant predator threats in the open fields and forced *Homo sapiens* to learn how to cope with the predators and adapt various means of survival techniques that allowed to form a social group branded together to fight against the predators. This survival instinct also made humans "intensely tribalist by nature" and developed a feeling "to belong to groups and, having joined, consider them superior to competing groups" (Wilson 2012, 290). Humans developed a strong desire to form in-group membership, and individuals prefer to mix and socialize with same groups of people, race, and other similar attitude, showing a tendency toward implicit racial bias in their behavior (Wilson 2012).

Discrimination is innate, but racism is power dependent.

The *Webster's New World Dictionary* defines *racism* as "a belief that race is the primary determinant of human traits and capacities and that racial differences produce an inherent superiority of a particular race" (Merriam-Webster, n.d.) whereas, *Oxford University Dictionary* defines as "prejudice, discrimination, or antagonism directed against someone of a different race based on the belief that one's own race is superior" (Oxford dictionary, n.d.).

These definitions are focused. A broad comprehensive definition is needed to expose the wide scope of the word *racism* where the influence of power plays a major role. It is defined as "ingroup members with the position of power discriminate outgroup members without status and privileges, which creates an atmosphere that lead to hostility, hate, and a sense of fear against the outgroup members." There are two types of racism—the non-conscious and conscious. The non-conscious racism is innate and guided by our amygdala, which detects external environmental threats and controls the body responses necessary to cope with the threat that can be real or perceived. This non-conscious racism is rooted in our survival instinct. Non-conscious racism is an essential component of threat detection system and conserved throughout mammalian evolution.

The conscious racism is a process guided by our neo-cortex of the brain that intentionally uses the position of power and/or privileges that allow the imposition of superiority and domination over the outgroup members. Exploitation and subjugation is the essence of conscious racism among human race. Conscious racism is present among all humans as long as differential power structures exist.

Modern humans use their non-conscious (implicit) response to outgroup individuals as a threat and change that responds through their conscious bias for their own benefit that comes from their power or advantage over individuals who are not privileged to similar status or power. This is true racism responsible for various types of abusive, hurtful, prejudicial, and dominating behavioral attitude inflicted upon out-group members. People privileged to have controlling authority over other groups of individuals exert superiority over subordinate, in all walks of life in economical, educational, and social context.

Even though all humans are racist, there are some dominating groups who abuse and extend biases to gain undue advantage over people who are their subordinate. Poor and weak individuals and groups hold their biases for short period, because they are hopeless and powerless. The victims give in to the demands and accept their sufferings and maltreatment with no protest.

Amygdala and non-conscious racism: Role of neurobiology

Amygdala, a small group of nuclei located bilaterally in the anterior temporal lobe acts as the main brain region involved in implicit emotional learning and memory, and, the perception of the automatic sensory stimulus (Stanley et al. 2008, Phelps and LeDoux 2005). Amygdala is the part of the brain that detects threats and controls the body responses necessary to cope with the threat through the process of non-conscious activity (i.e., without the knowledge of our consciousness). It is a part of the threat detection system (LeDoux 2002, 2015).

An external environmental danger signal processed through the visual and auditory pathways projected through amygdala is capable of detecting the threat and activating the unconscious process to prepare the individual to cope with the perceived or real danger through complex physiological changes in the body to deal with the threat, called fight or flight response. Amygdala sends distress signal to the hypothalamus, which triggers the sympathetic adrenal medullary axis (SAM) pathway, where the chromaffin cells of the adrenal medulla release hormones epinephrine and norepinephrine (also known as adrenaline and noradrenaline) directly in the bloodstream. Release of these two hormones causes massive physiological changes to prepare the individual for fight-or-flight response. Physiological changes involve increased heart rate and rapid breathing, which increases blood flow to muscular tissue, particularly the cardiac muscle and blood vessels. Increased cardiac output, blood pressure, and release of glucose from the liver help generate massive ATP synthesis, which gives the individual a burst of unlimited energy supply essential to cope with the threat. All these physiological activities taking place within a few seconds since the amygdala detect external environmental danger signal. Amygdala activation and its physiological control circuit have kept humans alive and survive the danger from predators for eons (Reece et al. 2014).

Humans develop attitudes that guides their judgment and behavior, whether positive or negative toward a specific concept, idea, ideology, or action (Grinnell 2016).

This attitude development is influenced by two distinct parameters such as non-conscious and conscious experiences. Non-conscious attitude is also known as implicit attitude, whereas conscious attitude is called explicit attitude. According to Greenwald and Banaji (1995), the definition of implicit attitude is, "intro-spectively unidentified (or inaccurately identified) traces of past experience that mediate favorable or unfavorable feeling, thought, or action toward a social object" (8). A phrase "traces of past experience" of the above definition provides important information regarding an assumption that lifetime experiences are the origin of implicit attitude, or would that be the origin during the human evolution?

Implicit attitude triggers automatically without our awareness and do not depend upon social context (Blair 2002, Fazio et al. 1995, Greenwald and Banaji 1995). As well, they are pervasive and found in all demographic groups (Nosek et al. 2007).

Research studies involving neuroimaging and other advanced techniques identified how we process race group information in our brain. Four areas of the brain have been implicated for regulating the process of information gathering and analysis of race-related activities such as amygdala, anterior cingulate cortex (ACC), the dorsolateral prefrontal cortex (DLPFC), and the fusiform gyrus, commonly known as the fusiform face area (FFA) (Kubota et al. 2012). These four areas work together to recognize faces, categorize them, and process how to react with each other (Gieg 2015–2016).

Hidden brain through evolutionary selection developed a preference to recognize human faces over other objects of interest. Human infants are capable of recognizing the faces of their parents, creating a strong bond that ensures they receive food, nourishment, affection, and security, guaranteeing their survival (Umilta et al. 1996). According to Bushnell (2001), it takes barely five hours of face-to-face time to develop a preferential attachment to a mother's face over other strangers around the infant. This innate preferential recognition of human faces, particularly parents, was "designed to be biased, to pay attention to faces at the expense of other objects, and to some faces at the expense of others," which assures the survival of the child (Vedantam 2010, 61–62).

Majority studies regarding "black white race attitude, beliefs and social decision making," focused on amygdala, a small almond-shaped structure that plays an important role for the acquisition, storage, and expression of fear conditioning and emotional learning and memory (Kubota et al. 2012). Research by Phelps & Thomas (2003) found that when Whites are shown images of Black faces, significant activation of amygdala occurred during functional magnetic resonance imaging (fMRI) experiments, whereas, when Black participants saw images of White faces, amygdala activation remained with the baseline, showing no significant changes.

Amygdala is critical for fear learning because of its implicit "physiological expression of emotional responses to neutral stimuli when paired with an aversive stimulus" (Stanley et al. 2008). Hart et al. (2000) reported that their study was "explicitly designed to assess fMRI responses to outgroup v. in-group faces across subjects of both races," and they found that initially no significant differences in amygdala activity were encountered between in-group and out-group faces. However, when subjects were scanned a second time after some rest period, the authors observed a decrease in amygdala activation for in-group faces than out-group faces, indicating a higher level of habituation effects for the in-group individuals. However, Phelps et al. (2000) provided a different interpretation of this experimental data. They suggested that this in-group–out-group differences in the amygdala activation response could be linked with a racial bias toward the members of out-group individuals.

White participants were exposed to unfamiliar Black and White faces during fMRI scanning process. After the completion of the imaging session, participants completed both explicit (Modern Racism Scale) and implicit (Implicit Association Test, IAT) which measures the racial attitude. The results revealed that the White participants with most negative implicit attitudes toward Blacks exhibited greatest difference in amygdala activation. These findings suggest that amygdala and behavioral responses of White participants to Black versus White faces reflect cultural group-level evaluation (Phelps et al. 2000).

Sumner (1906) explained the idea and importance of social "in-groups and outgroups" in his book *Folkways.* Humans have a propensity to stick with their own ethnic group (in-group) and develop a strong bond among the members of the same ethnicity. Ethnocentric ideas are based on the need for survival during the time of hominoid evolution. Our brain is trained to identify whether or not someone belongs to the same group. If it encounters a person perceived by the amygdala as an outsider, and does not belong to the in-group, then the amygdala would trigger the automated fight or flight response. This unconscious threat response system can be construed as implicit racism. Some researchers believe humans are born with a genetic predisposition to learn to fear people who are not members of the same social group. Olsson and colleagues (2005) proposed "millennia of natural selection and a lifetime of social learning may predispose humans to fear those who seem different from them."

Children with a genetic condition called Williams syndrome show friendly behavior even with absolute strangers because these individuals do not possess any sense of fear. These children were shown a series of images of various racial groups and asked to assign positive or negative features to each individual in the picture. Santos and colleagues (2010) observed that children with Williams syndrome showed no racial bias, whereas other children typically assigned each picture positive when features look like them (own), and negative when the features do not look like them (other races).

To understand the nature of amygdala response to racial difference, Lieberman and colleagues (2005) used fMRI technique in a study involving Caucasian and African-American individuals. Each participant looked at pictures of African-American and Caucasian-American faces during fMRI screening to examine the differential responses in amygdala. The result showed greater amygdala activities in the brains of Caucasian-American subjects when they were looking at the African-American faces. African-American subjects also exhibited higher amygdala activities when they were looking at African-American faces. But both African-American and Caucasian-American subjects showed no increased amygdala responses when they were looking at Caucasian-American faces. Lieberman et al. (2005) concluded that "present study suggests that the amygdala activity typically associated with race-related processing may reflect culturally learned to negative association regarding African American individuals." This study also suggested that increased amygdala response when looking at African-American faces might be a result of implicit behavioral response. Both racial groups (African and Caucasian Americans) perceived African-American faces as a threat, which could nurture an unconscious racial bias against African-Americans.

Researchers used propranolol—a drug prescribed for controlling hypertension, anxiety, and panic attacks—to study if propranolol could block our implicit racial bias. This study hypothesized that as propranolol is a beta blocker and can inhibit the action of adrenaline and other stress hormones on the sympathetic nervous system, then the implicit racism could be blocked by taking this drug. Caucasian students participated in this experiment and half of them took the drug and the rest took a placebo. Then each participant took the implicit attitude test (IAT), which measures implicit and hidden negative attitude toward social out-groups such as other races (non-whites) (Nosek et al. 2007). The results showed that students who took propranolol scored statistically lower scores for implicit/subconscious racism than students who received placebo. These results strongly suggest that by inhibiting students' autonomous fear reaction, drug propranolol significantly reduced implicit negative racial bias (Terbeck et al. 2012).

Racism: Sociopsychological basis

David Wellman defined racism as a "system of advantage based on race" (Wellman 1977). Whites enjoy access to better schools, housing, jobs, and other privileges because of social dominance. According to Beverly D. Tatum (1997, 7) racism means it will "allow us to see that racism like other forms of oppression, is not only a personal ideology based on racial prejudice, but a system involving cultural messages and institutional policies and practices and the beliefs and actions of individuals." Prejudice is a biased concept that develops in course of time because of incorporating various culturally induced stereotype, distortion of facts, intentional omission of truth, and derogatory comments to put someone down to a level of inferiority. These concepts development occurs as a result of the dominant group's forceful exertion over their subordinates. These cultural practices are ingrained in the society. Prejudice feeds the racism to flourish in a society where multiple types of population exist (Tatum 1997).

All heterogeneous populations carry this prejudicial culture. In some cultures it could be highly oppressive, and in some others it could be mild. But all people have their own prejudicial feelings. Social psychologists have observed that people have a tendency to form groups with people who have similar views. For example, people who have similar views about a football team such as the Denver Broncos will support each other, and like to spend time together. The group supporting the New England Patriots, on the other hand, will not like to mix with the members of the Bronco supporters. Both the groups show hatred toward each other. This hostility shows that "prejudice quickly established itself." The net result is, "in its power and universality, the tendency to form groups and then favor in-group members has the earmarks of instinct" (Wilson 2012).

The newborn infants show a preference to look at their mother's face and recognize it, showing that they have an inherited instinct.

In-group bias can also be inherited, which might "have arisen through evolution by natural selection (Wilson 2012, 59). The drive to form groups and propensity to be a part of that in-group membership is the part of tribalism, and people has a tendency to "prefer the company of others of the same race, nation, clan, and religion. They grow hostile to any outgroup encroaching upon the territory or resources of their in-group" (Wilson 2012, 60).

"Can people of color be racist?" When asked, Dr. Tatum answered that it depends on your definition of racism. "If one defines racism as racial prejudice, the answer is yes. However if one defines racism as a system of advantage based on race the answer is no. People of color are not racist because they do not systematically benefit from racism," and equally important, there is no "systematic cultural and institutional support or sanction for the racial bigotry of people of color" (Tatum 1997, 10).

Tatum believe the term "racist" only be reserved for "behaviors committed by whites in the context of a White dominated society is a way of acknowledging ever-present power differential afforded whites by the culture and institutions that make up the system of advantage and continue to be enforced notions of White superiority" (Tatum 1997, 10).

The unconscious brain controls the implicit racism and the conscious brain can modify the action of the unconscious, automatic responses, so that the outcome of the action is a positive response. Research evidence suggests that implicit racism is based on unconscious activities of the brain, which is malleable and dependent on both situational and dispositional factors (Blair 2002, Dasgupta 2009). However, explicit racism is under the power of the brain's conscious activities, and perhaps not malleable because individuals are totally brainwashed by their feelings of hatred and superiority that are culturally ingrained in their conscious existence, and that intense negative feelings on individuals, out-groups or any other human entity that could never be erased or compromised. This intense socially constructed racial prejudice has been metamorphosed into a force that killed the human decency and the essence of humanity that existed in all human beings. Racism is not restricted among various ethnicity or cultural groups, but it has taken a new form of existence that could wage a war resulting in the annihilation of the human existence on this planet.

Why does the black face evoke fear?

According to Wilson (2012), modern groups of humans are psychologically similar to the tribes of ancient history, and prehistory and direct descendants from the band of primitive pre-humans. Each tribe's desire to survive and prosper involved the art of war through intergroup aggression that has been documented in chimpanzee. The prehistoric tribal war among human tribes has been controlled by amygdala of the brain. All the fighting tribes were dark-skinned and they have incorporated dark-skinned human as the fear conditioning stimulus.

Intergroup aggression among nonhuman primates such as chimpanzees leads to lethal attacks by the male from one group to the males of the other group because of reproductive interest. The lethality of this aggression comes from the fear factor. It is possible that humans have evolved to fear others who do not belong to their social group and more likely who pose threats to them.

Scientists explained that blackface image triggers amygdala response, because Blacks have been portrayed negatively and sometimes as violent people, which creates a fearful response. The reason for this negative outcome is based on centuries of negative cultural associations regarding African-Americans—as second-class, inferior human beings. As all humans are *Homo sapiens*, our identity came from a diverse, multi-shaded melanin pigment-infused human entity, originating from the African mother eons ago. So, first members of *Homo sapiens* were dark skinned infused with heavy melanin pigmentation. Thus, dark-skinned faces were the images of all *Homo sapiens* at the dawn of human evolution.

The fear of black people has been present since the beginning of human evolutionary origin. Africa is the birthplace for *Homo sapiens*. At the beginning, all early humans were dark-skinned people. As one tribe tried to subjugate the other tribe so they could expand their living space and secure food resources, that was necessary for survival and evolutionary force dictated that behavior among tribes. In-group tribes stick together and help each other so that the tribe can flourish. Anybody who was not a member of the tribe was considered an out-group member and thus a threat and enemy. This in-group–out-group dynamic was regulated by the amygdala of the brain, which has played a significant role in our survival since the time of human origin.

This author, however, presents a different hypothesis that is not dictated by the social influence. When both Black and White exhibited activation of the amygdala when seeing the images of a Black person, it is possible that Blacks and Whites both fear the blackface, because our primitive amygdala is "remembering" or "recollecting" the episodes of prehistoric times when fear was provoked by seeing a different tribe member or out-group who was a dark-skinned person. Shades of black were predominate during early hominoid evolution. The loss of pigmentation and mutation in melanin-producing genes came much later date.

Racism: Effects on law and legal system

Young black men have been portrayed as violent, criminal, and dangerous (Trawalter et al. 2009). Black men have been implicitly as well as explicitly shown biased association with perceived threat (Payne 2001, Maner et al. 2005, Cottrell, and Neuberg 2005).

Negative culturally learned in-group–out-group bias may not fully explain that Black men are more looked upon as out-group members perceived as dangerous, and exhibit amygdala activation during facial fMRI studies. Richeson et al. (2008) suggested that Black men might be generating a stimulus that is signaling threat or danger to the participants during the fMRI facial image studies, which resulted in greater amygdala activation for Black faces. The results revealed that eye-gaze direction moderates race-related amygdala activity. Black targets only generated greater amygdala activity than White targets when the faces bore direct gaze.

Social psychologists have documented the stereotype of Black Americans as violent and criminal. The association between Blacks and crime is not only strong but also automatic (Payne 2001, Payne et al. 2002).

Correll et al. (2002) found during video game simulation that armed Black targets were shot much faster than armed White targets by the participants regardless of their racial attitudes. Eberhardt et al. (2004) found that unarmed innocent Blacks become the targets of "intense visual surveillance" by police officers because the eyes of officers perceived the Black targets as a group-based suspicion indicating stereotypic association on visual perceptual processes.

Implicit perceived threat of Black young men might play a role in the mind of law agency personnel in America. Recent shootings of unarmed young Black men by police officers might be influenced by the amygdala activity. It is conceivable that when a White police officer comes across a young Black man, and gazes at the Black man, the White officer might unconsciously perceive this encounter as a possible threat, which might influence his judgment of action, and cause him to use lethal force against the Black young man. This horrific action taken by the police officer can only be prevented if the police officers are routinely trained to the scenario of encountering Black young men so that they habitually develop a routine of seeing Black faces, and take a few seconds to cool down the unconscious fight/flight response. This training can help make conscious mind overtake the judgment of action that would prevent using lethal action.

The American judicial system is rigged with implicit racism. The majority of our judges in the court system are White and they give maximum sentences to young Black men committing a crime. The reason for this is based on the fear against Black young men, unconsciously controlling the value and judgment of the White judges. This unconscious racism actually influenced the judge to give a maximum punishment. White criminals with similar offenses will receive a more lenient punishment from a judge because in the judge's unconscious mind, the White criminal does not appear as a threat to them. This implicit racism in American judicial system is flourishing in every state of the Union.

CHAPTER 5

Segregation and Its Impact on Schools

The Supreme Court decision in *Brown v. Board of Education* outlawed segregated education in 1954. Since then school desegregation efforts to provide more equal educational opportunities to students have been rolled back through a series of judicial decisions (Orfield et al. 2012). During the 1990s the Supreme Court decision allowed schools systems to abandon desegregation and return to segregated neighborhood schools (*Freeman v. Pitts*, 503 U.S. 467, 1992 as cited in Orfield et al. 2012). Recent data from the Civil Rights Project show that school segregation based on economy and property is flourishing in United States. In the 2009–2010 school year, 74 percent Black and 80 percent Hispanic students attended schools where 50–100 percent of the students were a minority. Furthermore, at schools where 90 to 100 percent of the students were minorities, very few White and Asian students attended these schools (Orfield et al. 2012).

Public education is entrusted in our democratic society to lead, train, uplift, and provide educational equality and economic opportunities for all people. But various political barriers undermine these democratic idealisms in education. We have created a system of segregation that allows inequality to thrive in education and economic conditions. Creation of the school district in many states in the nation shows that often boundaries are drawn by the county administrators to contain poor families so that affluent areas will not intermix with poor, low-income communities. These economic segregation policies based on the value of local property wealth will keep affluent neighborhoods away from low-income neighborhood. The funds of the schools system are tied to the property tax, directly influencing the budget of the county/school district, which affect the type of schools built, the kind of facilities available, and the kind of instructional personnel to help students learn. All the strategic issues are controlled by revenue generated through property taxes.

Schools from the area where higher tax revenues are generated will have schools with modern buildings, facilities, and better educated instructional personnel with more rigorous curriculum and choices to select more advanced college preparatory courses for the students. The areas generating less revenue because of low property tax will have schools with marginal buildings, facilities and noncertified content area teachers, and almost non-existing advanced level college preparatory courses for the students. This inequality occurs between schools within the same school district because of economic segregation policies practiced throughout the US. Thus, this policy influences students' academic achievement.

The academic performance of eighth grade students representing schools with 10 percent poverty level scored on TIMSS mathematics test 557 points in 2007, whereas international test average was 500 (Gonzales et al. 2008).

In contrast, students from schools with over 75 percent poverty level scored 465 points (Table 1). In the year 2015 the math scores moved up to 573 points for students with less than 10 percent poverty level, whereas students representing 75 percent or more poverty level scored 477 points.

The average science scores in TIMSS examination of eighth-grade students in 2015 was 579 points for less than 10 percent poverty level, whereas 75 percent or more poverty level students scored 489 points (Table 2).

The results prove the point that well-endowed schools with better financial supporting system help to produce higher achieving students than schools, which are poorly funded. This system of educational disparity in the US perpetuates the academic caste system.

Table 1. Trends in average mathematics scores in TIMSS examination of eighth-grade students by school poverty level: 1999, 2003, 2007, 2011, and 2015.[7]

Level of Poverty in Percentage	1999	2003	2007	2011	2015
Less than 10%	546	547	557	533	573
10 to 24.9%	533	531	543	537	553
25 to 49.9%	495	505	514	519	531
50 to 74.9%	476	480	482	498	505
75 Percent or more	449	444	465	468	477

Table 2. Trends in average science scores in TIMSS examination of eighth-grade students by school poverty level: 1999, 2003, 2007, 2011, and 2015.[8]

Level of Poverty in Percentage	1999	2003	2007	2011	2015
Less than 10%	N/A	580	590	554	579
10 to 24.9%	N/A	567	567	552	563
25 to 49.9%	N/A	551	550	536	544
50 to 74.9%	N/A	519	520	515	519
75 percent or more	N/A	480	477	476	489

---

[7] Data taken from Figure 13 (TIMSS 2011) and Table 20 (TIMSS 2015). Provasnik, S., Kastberg, D., Ferraro, D., Lemanski, N., Roey, S., and Jenkins, F. 2012. Highlights from TIMSS 2011: Mathematics and Science Achievement of U.S. Fourth-and Eighth-Grade students an International context (NCES 2013-009 Revised), National Center for Education Statistics, Institute of Education Science, U.S. Department of Education, Washington, DC. TIMSS 2015, http://nces.ed.gov/timss/timss2015/timss2015_table20.asp.

[8] Data taken from Figure 13 (TIMSS 2011) and Table 42 (TIMSS 2015). Provasnik, S., Kastberg, D., Ferraro, D., Lemanski, N., Roey, S., and Jenkins, F. 2012. Highlights from TIMSS 2011: Mathematics and Science Achievement of U.S. Fourth-and Eighth-Grade students an International context (NCES 2013-009 Revised), National Center for Education Statistics, Institute of Education Science, U.S. Department of Education, Washington, DC. TIMSS 2015, http://nces.ed.gov/timss/timss2015/timss2015_table42.asp; not available.

SAT mean scores for college-bound seniors in critical reading, mathematics, and writing through 2001 to 2015 school years are presented in Table 3. There is a continuous decline in these scores by college-bound seniors. Reports show similar decline in average scores and international rank in science, reading, and mathematics in the PISA assessment for fifteen-year-old students in the US. In mathematics in the year 2015 US, a student's average score was 470 and international ranking of 37 (Table 4). This created a crisis because mathematics is the basis for all scientific studies and prosperity, innovation and technology.

Table 3. SAT mean scores of college-bound seniors: Selected years 2000–01 through 2014–15 (Re-centered Scale)[9]

School Year	Critical Reading Scores	Mathematics Scores	Writing Scores
2000–01	506	514	-
2001–02	504	516	-
2002–03	507	519	-
2003–04	508	518	-
2004–05	508	520	-
2005–06	503	518	497
2006–07	502	515	494
2007–08	502	515	494
2008–09	501	515	493
2009–10	501	516	492
2010–11	497	514	489
2011–12	496	514	488
2012–13	496	514	488
2013–14	497	513	487
2014–15	495	511	484

---

[9] Data from Table 226.10, U.S. Department of Education, National Center for Education Statistics (2016). Digest of Education Statistics, 2015 (NCES 2016-014). Retrieved from: https://nces.ed.gov/fastfacts/display.asp?id=171

Table 4. Average scores and rank of fifteen-year-old students from US on PISA tests in science, reading, and mathematics: 2000, 2003, 2006, 2009, 2012, and 2015.[10]

Year	2000	2003	2006	2009	2012	2015
Subject	Av. Score/ Rank	Av. Score/ Rank	Av. Score/ Rank	Av. Score/ Rank	Av. Score/ Rank	Av. Score/ Rank
Science Literacy	X X	X X	489 17	502 19	497 23	496 19
Mathematics Literacy	X X	483 X	474 32	487 24	481 30	470 37
Reading Literacy	504 X	495 X	X X	500 10	498 20	497 15

Concentration of poverty in a school has a greater negative influence on the students' achievement than their own poverty status (Borman and Dowling 2010). There is a direct relationship between student academic achievement and neighborhood property rate (Jargowsky and El Komi 2011). Students who attend high poverty, high minority–segregated schools receive low quality instructional and academic support services, produce student graduates with lower educational achievement, which limits their lifetime opportunities and progress (Mickelson 2006). The dropout rate in these poor schools is higher as well (Balfanz and Legters 2004).

The US has the highest incarceration rate in the world. "The scale of incarceration is measured by a rate that records the fraction of the population in prison or jail on an average day" (Western and

---

[10] This table represents a modification of Table 4 in performance of US fifteen-year-old students in science, mathematics, and reading literacy in an International context (NCES 2017-048). Data source: Organization for Economic Cooperation and Development (OECD), Program for International Student Assessment (PISA), 2000, 2003, 2006, 2009, 2012, and 2015. Also, selected findings from PISA-2012, 2015. Retrieved from https://nces.ed.gov/surveys/pisa/pisa2015/pisa2015highlights_1.asp

Petit 2010). From 1920s through mid-1970s about one hundred per one hundred thousand people were incarcerated, but since 1980 through 2008, the incarcerated rate jumped from 221 to 762 per one hundred thousand people. This explosive growth provides a dark picture about the social conditions we are experiencing where the race, age, education, and poverty are the thrusting force.

The incarceration rate in 2008 for men aged twenty to thirty-four who completed high school rose slightly from year 1980 among Whites, Latinos, and African-Americans to percentage points of 2.0, 2.5, and 9.0 respectively. However, in 2008 the data from men aged twenty to thirty-four who were high school dropouts showed an explosive growth of incarceration: Whites (13%), Latinos (7%), and African-Americans (37%) (Petit et al. 2009).

High school dropouts show almost 57 percent incarcerated rate for all men aged twenty through thirty-four during 2008. According to Bureau of Justice statistics in 2010, the US had at least 1.6 million prisoners in jail, so 912,000 young people aged twenty to thirty-four years were in jail. The majority of these people will not get jobs because of the social stigma of incarceration. Lack of technical skills forced them to depend on social welfare system/public assistance programs. They will again be a pernicious victim of a poverty cycle where there is no escape route.

Segregation in schools and its impact

Bernstein (1971) reported that the consequences of different cultures at home and school but particularly, the kinds of language used in both these places influence the learning abilities of children. For example at home, the language used is a "restricted code," where the language is short and sweet and creates an implicit understanding between the speaker and the listeners. In the school atmosphere, children use the "elaborated code," which is highly structured, filled with more "sophisticated words" for expression, and a strict format how to talk, how to behave, what to do, and how to conduct oneself. All these regimented languages suppress the originality and freedom of expression of these individuals, which is too mechanical and restrictive for learning.

Children from a low socioeconomic class suffer irreparable damage cognitively, because these children are not familiar with or have limited experience with the elaborated code when they go to school. They feel alienated and turned off from everything they are exposed to in the school. They develop a mental block that suppresses their ability to learn. To them, learning is a meaningless exercise that results in withdrawal, opting out, or very poor achievement outcomes. The middle-class children have experienced both the "restricted" and "elaborated" codes so they are capable of switching between one and the other, which ensures a successful outcome for these children (Bernstein 1973).

Willms (1999) reported that when students are segregated because of classes or tracks within schools, the disadvantaged students perform poorly.

CHAPTER 6

Caste System and Academic Slavery

The fundamental basis of creating the caste system was to develop an efficient system of governance of the society where each person contributes their best efforts and talent so that the society can perform and act as a unit. Each person has a specific job or trade where he/she can excel. This way each person can contribute his/her best intellectual productivity to the society, feel they belong to the social structure, and perform an essential role in the efficient operation of the society. This inclusive ideology allowed a cohesive force that bound everybody into the caste system. The freedom of creating something valuable to the society and enjoying the pleasure of creating and sharing their work toward the good of the society merged the structure of caste system for centuries.

Four major classes are developed based on their expertise in trades, practices, abilities, and talents as follows:

1. Brahmins—priestly classes, an expert in Vedas, performs various religious rites, and interprets the divine knowledge and preserve traditions.
2. Kshatriyas—warrior class, by tradition protects people from external and internal forces creating strife and endangering the operation of the society. The king and rulers belong to this class.
3. Vaisyas—this class represents merchant and business entrepreneurs who deal with money matters and many involved in lending money to individuals to jump-start businesses

and other endeavors needed to run social activities within a society.

4. Shudras—mainly labor class responsible for doing physical work that sustains all activities such as maintaining agricultural productivity through cultivation of the land, animal husbandry, and other menial jobs.

Beside these four classes within the caste system, another group of people also played a major role in the society known as Chandalas. These individuals belong to the lowest tier of Shudras who worked as hunters, butchers, and cleaners of human waste (Jayaram, n.d., Despande 2010).

Kshatriyas used their power and authorities to subdue the masses, and were always dependent on the support from the religious leaders, as the Brahmins represented the wishes of the gods. All cultures around the globe were influenced by the alliance between the religious leaders and warrior rulers, and this mystical hegemony ruled the whole human race for thousands of years.

The holistic and inclusive philosophy of labor structure that enhanced cohesiveness in social function was hijacked by the Brahmins representing the intellectuals, and they created a new power structure so they could control the whole caste in collusion with the rulers. This Brahmin-Kshatriya axis created a new interpretation of the caste system, where they could exert absolute control of the masses and impose their will. According to new interpretation, the highest caste belonged to Brahmin who controlled the entire religious affairs of the society, and they are the only ones who can deliver the teaching and learning of the God's wishes because the divine force has chosen Brahmins as the liaison between God and man. The Brahmins with the support of the king spread this socio-cultural-religious dictum and brainwashed the masses. Most of them were illiterate because of the social structure based on simple living.

Caste System in Secondary School

After desegregation in America, the secondary school system developed a new subtle caste system based on economic output of the county. The schools in the inner city are poor because most high-paying jobs and businesses left the city, relocated, or moved abroad. The inner city is abandoned and infrastructure of industrial, manufacturing jobs lost to foreign competition. Now the inner city is financially broke, which forced the schools to be malnourished and poverty-induced damages made schools academically dysfunctional. The suburbs flourished because high-earners and businesses moved there, which provided a financial boon to the school districts. This financial stability allowed the school administrators to build new, well-endowed secondary schools with better advanced curriculum, infrastructures, and better trained teachers. These schools offered large members of Advance Placement courses and college-level preparatory trainings which allowed the graduates to be better prepared and achieved higher intellectual attainment and productivity. This unequal distribution of wealth and opportunity created a clear caste system of Brahmins (the prepared, academically centered products), whereas, the inner city secondary schools produced poorly trained graduates who are handicapped (the Sudras - lower caste achievers). Thus by unequal wealth distribution created a solid, cultural, and intellectual barrier among its people and continuing the perpetual racial exploitation and flourishing caste system that is permeating through the heart of American education.

Caste System in Post-Secondary Education

American post-secondary educational institutions follow a caste system in their recruiting practices for faculty and administrative positions. The ranking of each institution is evaluated and maintained. If for any reason an institution dropped its ranking order, then a massive internal debate ensued involving the board of trustees and president to see what needed to be done to move the ranking up. Many distinguished presidents lost their jobs as a result.

Elite tier 1 universities represent the National Universities category where a full range of undergraduate and graduate programs are offered. These schools demand high intellectual productivity from its students. Groundbreaking research and innovations are expected from its graduates, and after graduation, these people will be selected for academic positions and become the faculty who would run day-to-day instructional, research, and other scholarly activities of the elite institutions. These tier 1 institutions include first twenty-five schools listed in the best National Universities in America published by US News and World Report (2018). These institutions produce the best intellectual, creative, and academic leaders in American educational enterprise.

Tier 2 universities occupy ranking ranging from 26 to 50 in the list presented by US News publication. These institutions produce the next best talents in academia. Tier 1 and 2 colleges and universities have the best available infrastructure for research, financial stability, and intellectual crossover linkage that can extract the best human quality and creativity from its products. They encourage creation of new ideas, technology, entrepreneurship, and other valuable assets for human race.

Tier 3 institutions are ranked between 51 through 75 in the list. The products of these institutions are the average academic performers who are the majority of the workforce in America. They are capable of doing excellent work, maintaining the economic engine and tackling the challenges of the twenty-first century. They are the mainstream workforce in American enterprise.

Tier 4 institutions hold the ranking from 76 to 150 in US News list. These educational enterprises cater to low-income, disadvantaged clienteles, providing homes and nurturing their talents to flourish in higher castes. Most of the products of these institutions survive the system and create a niche that supports the need of US workforce to run the economy and global demand for excellence.

Hiring practices for faculty positions among ranked universities and colleges follow the same pattern. Top 150 National Universities are predominantly White institutions (PWI) except for Howard University ranked 110. Historically Black Colleges and Universities (HBCU) follow a systematic caste system in hiring.

PWI will select candidates from tier 1–2 institutions who are mostly White for employment. However, these institutions will hire Black and Asian candidates from tier 1–2 institutions, who are productive scholars, and have the potential to contribute new knowledge to their respective fields of studies. They are considered equal to

White candidates. The racial influence plays a major role in academic sectors. Hiring practices in PWI are dictated by race even if it is illegal to do so according to federal guidelines. All institutions follow an unwritten rubric that is based on race to evaluate and analyze each prospective candidate for hire. White institutions want White faculty to teach their students because of the "role model" factor. The utility of the guise of "role model" has been plaguing the whole academia. White institutions will hire an Asian candidate only if the prospective candidate is at the level of genius through his/her intellectual maturity, scholarly productivity, and superior leadership qualities. The hiring institutions expect that chosen candidate will elevate the status of the university through the scholarly contribution of the person.

The unwritten racial requirement will be eliminated only through the outstanding scholarship of the candidate and the institution will benefit by acquiring a "Star." This also will help the institution show the world they are "color neutral" and believe in diversity. By hiring a minority, it is trying to fulfill the Federal government funding agencies requirement to have minority representation in the grant proposals and research activities. African-American scholars graduated from White universities like IVY-League institutions recruited by top-tier universities for faculty positions. They accept their positions and many receive special financial/infrastructural support from the universities in Science, Technology, Engineering, and Mathematics (STEM) areas. These additional perks are very important to selected faculties because of competitive cutthroat environments that will dictate the progress of their career and lead them to discover new knowledge that will benefit the whole human race. The productivity of these selected scholars is the beacon of intellectual enlightenment and the hope and aspiration of entire African-American communities.

These productive African-American scholars will never accept a faculty position in top-rated Historically Black Colleges and Universities (HBCUs). The question is why? These scholars understand that by accepting a faculty position from HBCUs, it will be the end of their career of intellectual growth, productivity, and enlightenment. It will be a self- imposed intellectual isolation and intellectual hara-kiri.

A question arises. Why will it be an intellectual hara-kiri for these scholars? Academic and infrastructural environment is not conducive for growth and freedom of mind, which are essential for creating new knowledge, discovery, and progress. In humanities, some scholars might produce outstanding works of literature, art, and music, but it is almost impossible to do great discovery in the STEM fields if manpower like post-doctoral/technicians help; other infrastructural and strong financial resources are not available to the researchers. Facilities and resources are very limited in the HBCUs whether they are public or private institutions. Cutting-edge research and other important discoveries happen only in top-rated academic institutions.

Howard University and Morehouse School of Medicine are in the top-ranked research universities among HBCUs. Productivity of the research faculty when compared to top-ranked White universities, Howard occupies a rank 184 according to Forbes list among all American research universities (Forbes List; n.d.).

Nature Publishing Group ranked Howard University 404 for institutional research outputs during January 1, 2017–December 31, 2017 (Nature Index; n.d.).

Few Howard University faculty have published their works in journals such as *Science, Nature, Proceeding of National Academy of Sciences, Physical Review, Journals of Biological Chemistry, Cell,* and others. Also few patents have been awarded to Howard University.

Examination of the membership roster of National Academy of Sciences revealed only twelve members who are faculty members among all HBCU combined (Table 1). By looking at these hard data, HBCU institutions cannot compete with ranked PWI. This supports the notion that HBCUs do not have the manpower, financial resources, necessary faculties, and infrastructural support to excel in these types of academic competition. The academic environment in most private HBCUs is not conducive for very rigorous, challenging intellectual activities because of many problems created by the administration. The governance of the institutions is controlled by the administrators who are anti-faculty, and not willing to listen to faculty concerns. The majority of HBCU Presidents are very auto-cratic and behave like dictators.

Table 1. Ranking of HBCUs among the top two hundred
American Research Universities in the nation[11]

Name	National Rank	2013 Federal Research Expenditure (X $1000)	Member of National Academy of Science
Howard University	172	33,403	7
Morehouse School of Medicine	169	34,511	3
Florida A & M University	188	28,446	-
Jackson State University	195	27,285	-

Caste System and American Academic Slavery in Higher Education

The American graduate educational system is the most effi-cient, demanding, prestigious, and productive entity in the world. Graduate students from all over the world come to various American universities for their academic training in the fields of science, med-icine, and engineering (Table 2.). The world's elite students enroll in various universities to get doctorate degrees of their chosen fields, and after receiving their degrees, they receive temporary working permits to continue their training. These are the group of budding intellectuals known as postdocs. Postdocs are the driving force of

---

[11] Data collected from the annual report of the top American Research Universities. Retrieved from: https://mup.asu.edu/sites/default/files/mup-2015-top-ameri-can-research-universities-annual-report.pdf

American ingenuity, innovation, and creative genius that is keeping America as the most powerful country of the world. The new discovery of knowledge through research and creative thinking brings an innovative spirit that propels to construct new technology. By using these new technological breakthroughs, they can create new products in medicine, engineering, agricultural, and other important areas, which in turn increases prosperity and healthy living. American prosperity and technological advancement is carried on the shoulders of postdocs and America should recognize and embrace their contribution as an essential component of American greatness and power. Unfortunately, this group of postdocs is living in a shadow of darkness where their lives do not matter, and almost in seclusion from the society. They do not have a voice to say anything; they live a life of intellectual slavery.

American research universities produce many doctorates in science, engineering, and health every year. The majority of graduate students come from foreign countries all over the world. These foreign students are the best products of their country of origin. American trained foreigners receive their doctorate degrees and they stay here to do their post-doctoral studies. Besides these American trained foreign postdocs, hundreds of foreign-trained postdocs are also granted temporary appointments in research at various research intensive universities.

Foreign students and foreign university-trained research scientists come to America because of opportunities and creative freedom. The American idealism of democracy and freedom of self-expression are absent in most countries. This attraction is the driving force that encourages the brilliant academic minds of young budding intellectuals to come to America and get further academic trainings in sciences and health-related disciplines. American elite universities follow a simple strategy that lure these young minds to get training here. The academia provides a stipend to cover the living expenses, adequate cutting-edge research facilities and infrastructural support, and unparalleled freedom of intellectual expression and creativity. This institutional support allows young minds to unleash their intellectual productivity that translates into innovative and technological breakthroughs. As a result institutions can earn patents, status, and other tangible benefits like monetary and intellectual property.

Table 2. Graduate enrolment in science and
engineering fields 2009–2014[12]

Characteristics	2009	2010	2011	2012	2013	2014
Science and Engineering (a)	545,685	556,532	560,941	561,418	570,300	601,883
Full time	398,498	409,107	411,168	414,384	424,508	447,096
Male	307,936	316,051	318,209	318,870	324,913	348,390
Female	237,749	240,481	242,732	242,548	245,387	253,493
US citizen/Permanent Resident/Full time	256,503	263,871	262,043	258,477	256,211	253,886
Hispanic or Latino	27,265	28,609	30,808	31,406	32,819	35,132
Asian	31,754	32,185	33,147	32,700	32,917	33,745
Black or African-American	29,973	31,094	32,197	31,338	30,911	30,482
White	250,443	255,256	256,096	250,783	246,518	245,103
Unknown race/ethnicity	36,933	34,682	30,409	28,430	26,965	25,701
Temporary visa holders/Full time	141,995	145,236	149,125	155,907	168,297	193,210

The postdoctoral appointments in American universities provide a stipend that is usually funded by the government agencies

---

[12] Survey of graduate students and post-doctorates in science and engineering. National Science Foundation, National Center for Science and Engineering Statistics (NCSES). Info Brief, NCSES March 2016 (Revised) NSF 16-310. Table 1.

such as National Institutes of Health (NIH), National Science Foundation (NSF), Department of Defense (DOD), Department of Environmental Science, and other agencies.

Every year one hundred thousand postdoctoral appointments are available for applicants. The duration of appointments ranges from (1–5) years. Depending upon the area, most appointees are foreign born postdocs as a limited number of American-born postdocs apply for these positions (Table 3).

Table 3. Postdoctoral appointees in science, engineering, and health fields by sex, citizenship, race, and ethnicity: 2010–2014.[13]

Characteristics	2010	2011	2012	2013	2014
Science and Engineering	44,320	44,121	43,841	43,395	44,623
Male	28,531	28,314	28,176	27,858	28,618
Female	15,789	15,807	15,665	15,537	16,005
US citizen and Permanent Residents	20,430	20,340	20,214	20,257	20,453
Hispanic or Latino	813	901	862	961	1,020
Asian	3,592	3,502	3,330	3,526	3,489
American Indian/Alaska native	62	66	51	71	65
Black or African American	564	610	615	667	702
Native Hawaiian or other Pacific Islander	53	53	63	50	53
White	11,980	11,965	11,835	11,953	11,994
Unknown ethnicity and race	3,285	3,082	3,346	2,864	2,962
Temporary Visa Holders	23,890	23,781	23,627	23,138	24,170
Health	19,119	18,518	19,010	18,547	18,970

[13] Survey of Graduate students and Post doctorates in Science and Engineering. National Science Foundation; National Center for Science and Engineering Statistics InfoBrief: NCSES, March 2016 (Revised) NSF-16-310.

Total postdoctoral appointments in Science and Engineering from the years 2010–2014 averaged about 44,060 positions each year (Table 3.). The postdoctoral appointments earned by US citizens and permanent residence on average was 20,339 during this time period. Temporary visa holders earned postdoctoral positions on average 23,721 for the same period. Temporary postdocs are over 3382 positions on average over US citizens and permanent residents combined, showing that the research in Science and Engineering deeply depends on temporary postdoctoral hands and brains. These symbiotic intellectual interactions between US trained scientists and foreign-born scientists pushed American research productivity, and innovative outputs into a level of extraordinary achievements that brought groundbreaking scientific discoveries in the fields of biomedicine, computer science and engineering, chemistry, physics and other science and engineering fields (Table 3a.).

Table 3a. Postdoctoral appointees in selected
subfields of Science: 2010-2014*[14]

Characteristics	2010	2011	2012	2013	2014
Science	37,351	37,335	36,738	36,289	37,316
Agriculture	1,190	1,256	1,290	1,319	1,402
Biological Sciences	21,726	21,107	20,086	19,330	19,554
Computer Sciences	763	759	760	765	834
Earth, Atmospheric and Ocean Sciences	1,740	1,774	1,956	2,032	2,061
Mathematics and Statistics	791	830	902	932	959
Physical Sciences	7,583	7,490	7,430	7,197	7,277
Psychology	1,132	1,124	1,132	1,023	1,066
Social Sciences	711	774	799	938	1,051
Other Sciences	1,715	2,221	2,383	2,753	3,112

---

[14] Survey of Graduate students and Post doctorates in Science and Engineering. National Science Foundation; National Center for Science and Engineering Statistics. InfoBrief: NCSES, March 2016 (Revised) NSF-16-310.

These pool of postdocs are "temporary workforce" supporting the American engine of innovation and technological progress. They work in their appointed positions for one to three years, or more, if grants are renewed and performance is satisfactory to the eyes of the principal investigator (PI). The PIs are professors who organize the project, and postdocs are the foot soldiers who do the actual work to execute the ideas delineated in the proposed proposal. The postdocs are the real pioneers and the main discoverers of the new knowledge, technique, or various concepts that come out of their creative minds. They work ten to twelve hours shift each day in the laboratory, sometimes longer, so that the new discoveries/ideas can come out from their secret hideouts and enlighten them.

The PIs are the managers who seldom work in the lab and act as the masters. Postdocs are the slaves. New discoveries or concepts that might prove very important for the progress of science receive extraordinary publicity and accolades, then the PI receives all the credit, but the postdoc responsible for this discovery gets a pat on the back and perhaps a few dollars in the pocket as a token of appreciation from the master. This kind of hypocritical and oppressive system is deeply rooted in academic research establishment. The professors know they do not deserve the credit but seldom announce that credit should go to the postdocs or graduate students involved in the research project. Because of this unwritten oppressive policy, sometimes graduate students/postdocs falsify data or manufacture non-existing procedures/techniques to take revenge against the existing dishonest, unethical practices that have been used in the institution.

Most postdocs know their chances to get a permanent faculty position are very slim, and this is insurmountable among foreign-born postdocs. These postdocs are the "roving refugees" move from one grant/one institution to another grant/another institution. They receive poor wages for their work and not competitive salaries for their academic training and experiences.

Many came to America to avoid oppression, economic stagnation, and curtailment of freedom of self-expression that engulfed their countries. But they are entrapped in new sets of oppression and economic stagnation and academic slavery that hide in the practices of academic establishment in America.

The Plight of Postdocs

Regardless of American-born or foreign-born postdocs, these people do not experience respectful or welcoming attitudes from the university administrative leaders or grant management sectors. The fiscal managers know postdocs are "trainees"; they receive a stipend but not a salary. This distinction between trainee and salaried personnel is critical as far as income for the university is a concern.

Funding agencies like the National Institutes of Health treat postdocs as "trainees" their stipends cannot be considered for the "Indirect Cost," and University loses a huge amount of money that institution would like to get. The "indirect cost" is the "free money that the university can use for any reason," even to buy a yacht for the president!

Postdoc stipends cannot earn indirect cost. Administrators look at the postdocs as nobody or invisible in the institutions. Postdocs can write proposals but cannot be principle investigators on a grant proposal, so PI, the mentor, is the master and postdoc is a slave. This intellectual slavery is rampant in ivory towers of the American research universities and institutes. Postdocs are the cheap labor force the academic institutions use to do research, develop a cure for various diseases, create a new technology that would revolutionize the industry, and other discoveries that drive the innovative and intellectual productivity of America, which allows the US to be the most powerful country in the world.

CHAPTER 7

Who Are We?

Birth of British Colonial America

Who are we?

The British colonialists envisioned the new colony of North America as a great opportunity to invest and develop this massive land mass for agricultural bounty and profit making with the help of expandable people—the so-called waste people, who would work day and night through their sweat and blood.

In the early days of settlement in America, this was the main motive for the rich British nobility to expand their influence and wealth, at the same time clean out the prisons filled with wretched criminals in London and around British Isles, and ship them to America. The unwanted people who were sent on the hazardous voyage to America (those who survived), served the interest of English nobility and colonialist. The "first comers," as they were known, were mostly common criminals and vagabonds. Many who disembarked from the Mayflower died in the first year because of starvation and scurvy—a disease caused by vitamin C deficiency (Isenberg 2016, 10).

Colonists were comprised of different people. The poor and criminals occupied the bottom layers, the next was indentured servants, "many of them choosing exile over incarceration in disease-ridden English prison," (Isenberg 2016, 13). Because of labor shortage, ship captains and their agents rounded up street children in London and other cities with the blessing from the authorities of British royalty, and sold them to the rich planters who were going to America. These boys and girls were bought by these rich planters so they could exploit these children as their indentured servants.

England had no legal institution for slavery, but with the support from the monarchy, the royal family invested in the African slave trade and sugar-growing colonies through the Royal African Company (Finkelman 2012). The British established a class system where rich, nobility, and wealth were the supreme order and the poor served the rich and powerful forever.

British colonists were easy working people. To encourage them and perhaps prevent racial impurity as these colonists were mixing with native Indian women, the British profiteers arrange shipment of White women to the colony. In 1620 the Virginia Company shipped fifty-seven "young, handsome, and educated maids" to Virginia. Over the next three years, 157 more women made the crossings. According to the company records, it provided a reason for sending these young women to the colonialist in Virginia. It stated "greatest hindrances" to "noble worker" rested on "want of comforts"; men deserved to "live contentedlie." The transportation of female cargo would "tye and roote the planter's myndes to Virginia by the bonds of wives and children. Sexual satisfaction and heirs to provide for would make slothful men into more productive colonists" (Isenberg 2016, 27).

Establishment of Slaves in British Colonial America

The ship *Mayflower* landed on Cape Cod in 1620. A mass migration of British people took place in 1630 when John Winthrop led a fleet of eleven ships carrying seven hundred passengers and livestock (Isenberg 2016).

Europeans planted the seeds of slavery in the British Colony of America in 1619, when Dutch colonialists brought the first African slaves to Jamestown, Virginia. The main reason to establish the institution of slavery was to clear the land and use the land for agricultural practices so that a good homestead could be built. Slave labor was used so that the planters could be rich and prosperous within a short period—planters who represented the elite class of English nobility, who did not know of agricultural practices, but knew their wealth can be made in this new world through agriculture. They brought with them their livestock so that in this vast land the livestock could flourish. African slaves were a cheap and plentiful labor force and a rugged group of men and women used to hard work. The European indentured servants were a class of people who were lazy and lethargic and unable to do hard labor for the planters. Thus, African slaves were the perfect choice.

Slavery spread throughout the British American colonies. Over eight million slaves were brought to the New World during the eighteenth century alone and many more in the nineteenth century (Slavery in America; 2009).

Daily Life of a Typical Slave

One hour before daylight, the sound of horns would awaken the slaves from their slumber. They gobbled their breakfast with corn cake and cold bacon pieces and ran to the cotton fields to pick cotton until sunset. They could take a break at noon for fifteen minutes to swallow their allowance of cold bacon for lunch. That was the only break they had before continuing cotton picking until the sunset. At sunset, each slave weighed his/hers picked cotton basket for the day and carried their basket load of cotton in the gin house. Each slave must pick same amount of cotton each day; if the weight of the cotton picking fell short from the established cotton picking capability, then the slave was not working hard enough in his/her duties, and he/she was lashed with the whip made up with rawhide strands that peeled skin and flesh by each blow of the whip (Northup 2014).

Day and night each slave feared the whipping routine and of oversleeping in the morning. If that happened, the punishment was a minimum of twenty lashes! Slaves worked yearlong in areas such as ploughing, planting seeds, picking cotton, corn, cleaning and pulling weeds and clearing the land to grow cotton, corn, sweet potato, and sugar cane. Also, slaves cultivated cabbage, fruits, and vegetables.

Slavery and Founding Fathers of America

John Locke authored the fundamental constitutions of Carolina in 1669, which proclaimed that "every freeman in Carolina shall have absolute power and authority over his negro slaves." Locke was the founding member of the Royal African Company who had gained monopoly rights to the British slave trade. King Charles II of England issued colonial charters to a group of influential British aristocracy as the "absolute lords and proprietors" and Locke was the private secretary of Lords proprietors. The fundamental constitution endorsed slavery and defined that power rested at the top of the aristocratic society, and emphasized that no democratic idealism was allowed (Isenberg 2016, 43).

George Washington along with William Byrd II wanted to drain dismal swamp that divided Virginia from Carolina so that recovered land could grow hemp for fiber and cut wood for housing. George Washington established a company in 1763 "whose purpose was to use slaves to drain the swamp" (Isenberg 2016, 48–49).

Thomas Paine published a book *Common Sense* in January 1776, where he marginalized slaves in his grand vision of the new world order.

Thomas Jefferson fathered several children with a slave Sally Hemings and believed in the breeding aspect of women. Women are more valuable and prized possession than men. Jefferson said "men might raise food, but it was quickly consumed; women produce children that could be sold as stock . . . I consider the labor of breeding women as no object, and a child raised every 2 years is of more profit than the crop of best laboring man." Further, he thought women were meant to breed, because "providence has made our interest and duties coincide perfectly" (Isenberg 2016, 100).

Many prominent Founding Fathers of America such as George Washington, Thomas Jefferson, John Hancock, James Madison, Benjamin Franklin, John Jay, Patrick Henry, and others owned many slaves and used them to run their agricultural enterprise and perform household chores. Founding fathers from northern states did not like slavery, but for the sake of maintaining unity among northern and southern state members represented in the Constitutional Convention of 1787, they allowed slaveholding states to keep slaves in their states (Laccarino n.d.).

This acquiescence by founding fathers regarding slavery was necessary to achieve the larger goal of securing the unity and independence of the United States. Thomas Jefferson wrote in the Declaration of Independence, "We hold these truths to be self-evident, that all men are created equal, that they are endowed by their creator with certain unalienable Rights that among these are Life, Liberty and the pursuit of Happiness" (The Declaration of Independence).

These words reflect what United States of America would be in the eyes of the world where freedom, justice, and democratic idealism flourish forever. The enslaved people from Africa would not be a part of this dream enshrined in the bosom of United States of America and their tears, blood, suffering, and shackles of injustice would continue for another century.

Thomas Jefferson blamed the British colonial policies for the slavery but "absolved the Americans of any responsibility for owning slaves themselves" (Laccarino n.d.).

After American independence in 1776, slavery prospered for another 175 years, in different forms and function. The brutality and inhumane suffering of the people has subsided but a new form of slavery in the guise of poverty through toxic stress has engulfed American society. The conflict of the "haves" and "have not" has been creating a fractured society where the idealism of the "Life, Liberty and the Pursuit of Happiness" is a mirage!

Revolutionary War and Slavery

The Revolutionary War started when Crispus Attucks, a Negro slave, led a group of men who charged against the British soldiers in the battle of King Street in Boston. He was killed by a bullet. His flowing blood in white snow wrote the first page of the history of American Revolution that would explode and create a new republic. John Adams, the second president of America said, "Not in the Battle of Lexington or Bunker Hill, Not the surrender of Burgoyne or Cornwallis were more important events in American history than the battle of king street on the 5th of March, 1770" (Bennett, Jr. 1962, 55).

Attucks, a Black slave, gave his life so that Whites could gain freedom from the British tyranny! Many Black slaves joined the war against the British army. When George Washington took command of American troops, an order came from his headquarters forbidding the enlistment of Negroes. (Bennett, Jr. 1962). The White young men avoided joining the Continental army of George Washington, and many of these young men deserted the army. The American government offered bounties such as land and money to lure young Whites to volunteer in the army. Washington was frustrated, and said, "Such a dearth of public spirit." George Washington took with him nine thousand men in December 1777 during the Valley Forge military operation, but by March 1778, over three thousand men deserted the military operation.

After the Valley Forge experience, George Washington realized that he needed help from Black slaves to join the Continental army. Black soldiers fought, and many gave their life for the freedom, which they never enjoyed during their lifetime. Almost 10 to 15 percent of Black soldiers served in the Revolutionary War, and they served in "almost every unit in every battle from Concord to Fort Ticonderoga to Trenton to Yorktown" (Collins 2013).

Hundreds of thousands of Negro slaves received their freedom because of the Revolutionary War, and thousands more ran away to Canada to achieve their freedom. The Declaration of Independence influenced many slave owners in the North to change their attitude toward slavery and release thousands of slaves to be free. The right of man movement was instrumental in breaking the shackle of slavery in the North and eliminated slavery for good. Through legislative decrees and court actions, Negro slaves became free men (Bennett, Jr. 1962).

Many people expected the death of slavery in the South would happen soon after the demise of the slavery in the North at the end of the Revolutionary War, but that did not happen. The invention of the cotton gin machine and the need for manpower that would revitalize the agricultural South prevented the demise of slavery in South.

Slavery and Reconstruction

An assassin's bullet took away the life of President Abraham Lincoln on the dreadful day of April 15, 1865. His death also snatched away the dreams of millions of African-Americans to achieve freedom and prosperity in their lifetime.

Andrew Johnson was the vice president, and he assumed the presidency after the death of Abraham Lincoln. President Johnson, who hailed from Tennessee, saw the destruction of the South's agricultural-based economy and infrastructure as a result of the Civil War and ensuing abolishment of slavery which would cause further misery and total paralysis of his White brethren. He was determined to save the Southern economy. Member states of the ex-Confederacy can join the union if they would abide by the directives of the federal government, which stipulated that former Confederate States must adhere to and uphold the abolition of slavery, swear loyalty to the Union, and pay off their war debt. President Johnson emphasized that he believed the rights of the states came first during the formation of the republic and believed federal government had no business in the internal affairs of each state (History.com; n.d. Andrew Johnson).

President Andrew Johnson realized that millions of poor Whites would be emancipated along with Negroes during the Civil War, and these poor Whites could be important resources for his own political agenda and cementing his own legacy as president. He said to the South Carolina delegation he would elevate "poor white man who struggled to till barren, sandy soil for subsistence, and who were look down upon by the Negro and elite planter alike" (Isenberg 2016, 178).

President Johnson was instrumental to dismantle the noble ideas inscribed in the Emancipation of Proclamation and raised a new level of racial discord that supported White supremacy. He was instrumental to remove the freed slaves' human right to engage in a civil society where each person can cast their votes, and select persons who would raise their concerns and present them in the Congress. Johnson's administration supported Southern Whites' demand to reestablish the White supremacy. He proclaimed in his annual 1867 message to Congress that "Negroes have shown less capacity for government than any other race of people . . . wherever they have been left to their own devices they have shown a constant tendency to relapse into barbarism." The "blacks of the South are utterly ignorant of public affairs that their voting can consist in nothing more than carrying a ballot to the place where they are directed to deposit it" (Johnson 1867).

President Johnson rescinded the orders that land confiscated from Confederates could not be given to the ex-slaves so they could build their own farms. All ex-Confederate States joined the union and sworn that they will abide by the US Constitution. Southern states believed in what President Johnson had said about the state rights, and they were busy in creating various plans of action that would bring back the glorious south again politically, economically, and culturally.

The Southern agricultural-based economy was in a shamble; thousands of freed slaves left the Southern states and moved to the safe environment of the Northern states where the ex-slaves would find safety and better job opportunities in fast-growing industrialization.

The Civil War was a bloody war, which destroyed Southern states representing the Confederacy. After the end of the Civil War, the federal government provided its resources to help to rebuild the South called the Reconstruction period which started in 1865 and ended in 1877. By late 1865, Congress passed the Thirteenth Amendment, which ended the institution of slavery. However, President Andrew Johnson, who espoused the states' rights over the federal government's rights in internal operation of the states, followed a lenient Reconstruction policy that allowed Southern states and White Southerners to take control of the Civil authority during 1865 and 1866, and enacted a series of state laws to curtail the ex-slaves' activities and use them as a cheap labor force to maintain their agricultural enterprise. These enacted state laws were known as "Black Codes." Many Southern States coerced ex-slaves to sign yearly labor contracts almost paying no wages and if any ex-slave refused to sign the labor contract, then he was arrested as a vagrant and fined or forced into hard labor for a long period. This oppressive law was imposed in all former Confederate States. In some states the authority imposed "anti-enticement" clause designed to prevent Blacks from moving from one plantation to the next. Anyone who offered higher wages to a Black laborer who was under a contract already would be punished financially, thus forcing the contracted laborer to stay in the same working place. Many planters abused their laborer physically as well as mentally. To avoid this brutal treatment by the owner, a good deal of ex-slaves wanted to run away to other places and look for other types of jobs (Wagner n.d.).

Because of the restrictive nature of the black codes and unfairness along with brutality caused outrage among Northern states, and they wanted to repeal Black codes. In the Congressional election of 1866, the Republican radicals won a majority and the radical wing of the Republican Party took control of the government. Black codes were repealed in 1866. The Republican Party initiated the Radical Reconstruction era in 1867 and passed the Civil Right Acts over President Johnson's veto in 1866. It also passed the Fourteenth Amendment (equal protection for former slaves) in 1868. The Fifteenth Amendment (the voting rights) approved by the Congress in 1870 empowered the Black voters to take part freely in the political arena of the US. Many freedmen got elected in the State legislature and the US Congress.

How sex altered the English common law and influenced the idea of a slave as property

According to the English common law, even one child born out of wedlock, the child will have the same rights as the father of the child, and the father has to provide support to raise this illegitimate child. The British settlers in Virginia involved in a sexual relationship with female slaves by force, or adulterous alliance, because of a shortage of British women in the colony, which resulted in many mixed race children. The leaders of Virginia devised a new legal instrument by adapting the Roman law where all offspring of livestock and domesticated animals born would be the property of the owner of the dam or female who gave birth. By treating the female slaves as property and placing them in a similar category as livestock, the White Virginian established coercive sexual practices on female slaves with no fear and legal consequences (Finkelman 2012).

In 1662, the White men in the House of Burgesses enacted a new law that stated all children born shall be held bonded or free only according to the condition of the mother. If the mother is a slave, then all children born would also be a slave (Finkelman 2012).

Throughout the American Revolution, the Southern politicians insisted that slaves were property rather than a person. The Constitutional Congress in 1776 adopted the Declaration of Independence and the allocation of taxes involving slaves created a deep rift between Northern delegates and Southern delegates. To support work of the new Central Government, each state had to contribute taxes based on population so that the operational cost of running the government could be equally shared by each state. Some Southern delegates raised the prospect that if Congress wanted slaves as people than property, then the Confederation might not be workable. The Northern delegates lost the debate and acquiesced to the idea that slaves were not people! (Finkelman 2012).

Jefferson wrote that all men are free, liberty and equality for all people who live in this land, but slaves were not included in that sentiment. There was enormous contribution of slaves for the nation building process, in the economic sectors of the agricultural enterprise were all forgotten. The interest of the slaves were completely neglected during the Revolutionary era, so that a constitution can be passed by the Congress, and the new nation would be born as the United States of America. For the sake of unity to maintain the Republic, the Whites agreed to ignore the slave's human existence. Slaves had to give up their identity as a part of human race, the dream of liberty, justice, and happiness.

The British evacuated the American colony along with over 15,000 slaves and gave them freedom to live as freemen. American

Republic demanded that British should return those slaves to America but British government offered monetary compensation for the lost slaves, and refused to hand over the slaves showing they valued more the freedom for slaves than the United States of America (Finkelman 2012). Lofty, utopian idealism inscribed in the Declaration of Independence, where freedom, liberty, happiness were the essence of the American identity, idealism, and core value, but for the slaves, liberty, justice, freedom, and pursuit of happiness were only slogans filled with broken promises and unfulfilled dreams like a mirage!

CHAPTER 8

A Short History of Black Education

Education is the primal force of human wisdom that guides us through natural barriers, obstacles, hindrances, and cradles the progress toward freedom, and practice the freethinking spirit of a civilized human being pursuing the ultimate—the truth. The emancipation of mind, body, and soul can only be achieved through education.

During slavery, the slave masters practiced butchery, dehumanization, torture, rape, and spiritual destruction of the minds of slaves and established a code of punishment if anyone showed an inclination toward knowledge through education that will provide a sense of uplift of the soul. The punishment of death was the ultimate price for the slaves to pay should they deviate from the code of servitude. Education was forbidden to these people so they could be bonded/shackled their entire life to ignorance, and the White masters could maintain their superiority.

Suppression of education allowed Whites to maintain their supremacy over Blacks and quell the fears of slave rebellions. Slavery was the economic engine of prosperity for White slave owners. They needed the manpower to maintain the agricultural enterprises in South, and to some extent in the Northern states of America.

In the North, some colleges opened their doors for black students to enroll and get an education. Oberlin College in Ohio was founded in 1833 and allowed the first Black student to enroll in 1835. Some Northern colleges and universities recruited talented Black youths so they could be trained as clerics and educated freed slaves and converted them to Christianity.

The first Black institution of higher learning was established in Pennsylvania through the philanthropy of Richard Humphrey, a Quaker in 1837. Quakers were against slavery and championed many social causes during this era. The first school was initially named as the Institute of Colored Youth (ICY) and the main purpose of this Institute was to train slaves in fundamentals of reading, writing, arithmetic, agriculture, mechanical arts, and other practical trainings so they could become literate and achieve economic solvency. After some years of operation, the Institute of Colored Youth changed its name to Cheyney University and the main goal was to prepare students to become teachers and help their fellow man (Cheyney University n.d).

White philanthropist John Maynard Dickey and his wife Sarah E. Cresson established Ashman Institute for Black men to train in science, classics, and theological education in 1853. In 1866, the institution was renamed Lincoln University in honor of the president Abraham Lincoln. The founder of the institution expanded the college into a full-fledged university to provide education in law, medical, pedagogical, and theological school besides College of Liberal Arts. Dickey graduated from Princeton University and was a strong believer of rigorous classical curriculum and strong ties with the Presbyterian Church.

He used the curricula of the Princeton University as the template for Lincoln University. The Lincoln University was the first Black institution to grant degrees. Graduates established seven other Black colleges and universities in the South.

Wilberforce University was founded in 1856 in Ohio and named after the eighteenth-century abolitionist William Wilberforce. It was a Methodist affiliated institution. Besides being an academic institution, the Wilberforce University played an important role in Ohio Underground Railroad system. The Civil War started in Charleston, South Carolina, on April 12, 1861. During the Civil War the enrollment went down and the college closed its doors in 1862. In July 10, 1863 the University reopened.

Christian abolitionists founded an educational organization called the American Missionary Association (AMA) in Albany, New

York, in 1846. The members of this organization believed slave holding was wrong, immoral, and an act of sin because all Blacks were members of the "equal brotherhood the family of Christ" (Williams 2006).

The American Missionary Association founded Atlanta University (1865), Fisk University (1866), Hampton Institute (1868), Tougaloo College (1869), Dillard University (1869), Talladega College (1867), LeMoyne-Owen College (1862), Tillotson/Huston-Tillotson University and Avery Normal Institute (1867).

Howard University in Washington, DC, was founded by AMA with the Freedman's Bureau in 1867 (DeBoer 1973). These institutions of higher learning were established by AMA so that Black leaders in education, science, medicine, engineers, and other notable professionals could be produced for future generations. In the beginning Historically Black Colleges and Universities (HBCUs) were established to provide elementary and secondary education to Black students.

During the Civil War (1861–1865) less than 5 percent of 4.5 million Blacks were literate (Brown 1999). In 1865, before the end of Civil War, only forty Black students graduated from colleges and universities and all of them were from Northern institutions (Black chronology; n.d.).

After the end of the Civil War in 1865, the US Congress established the US Bureau of Refugees, Freedmen, and Abandoned Lands popularly known as the Freedmen's Bureau to help former Black slaves and poor Whites in the South by providing food, medical aides, housing, and established schools during the Reconstruction era.

At the end of the Civil War, four million slaves gained freedom and needed to be educated so they could function in a democracy. The Freedmen's Bureau helped to build thousands of schools to accommodate millions of former slaves to get an education and trained thousands to gain industrial and agricultural skills. The Bureau also played an important role with the American Missionary Association and other charitable organizations to start off various Black institutions of higher learning like the Howard University, Fisk University, and Hampton University (History.com).

Justin Smith Morrill, a representative and a senator from Vermont, handled the enactment of the Morrill Acts of 1862. This bill mandated federal funding through land grants for the creation of many public colleges and universities in USA. Each eligible state received 30,000 acres of federal land for each member according to the census of 1860. Funds generated through the sale of this land were used to establish colleges and universities to teach agriculture, mechanic arts, military tactics, and liberal arts (Morrill Acts). These institutions of higher learning became land-grant colleges and universities (Morrill Acts of 1862 and 1890; n.d.).

At the end of the Civil War in 1865, over four million free slaves needed training in various trades such as agriculture, animal husbandry, industrial trades, and other useful professions. The segregated Southern states did not allow freedmen to get an education in these land-grant institutions. To rectify this situation, the Second Morrill Act in 1890 dictated that whenever a segregated White land-grant college would be established, a separate public land-grant college for Blacks must be created. These land-grant institutions focused on agriculture, mechanical and industrial studies (US Department of education 1991).

The Morrill Land-Grant Act of 1890 created public educational institutions emphasizing agricultural and mechanical training for former slaves. The second act created seventeen Historically Black land-grant colleges in Southern states (Morrill Acts).

After the end of the Civil War and the Reconstruction, America underwent economic transformation from an agricultural economy to a new powerful industrial economy. The second Industrial Revolution from 1870 and 1914 was fueled by the abundance of natural resources, innovations in transportation, and a growing labor force from European immigrants and freed slaves.

White industrialists realized that cheap labor was an important component in their wheel of industrial power and wealth. One of the best ways to get a continuous supply of a cheap labor force was to provide assistance and training to the emancipated Southern Blacks for industrial and agricultural trades. Newly founded Black colleges and institutes became the supply line for this job-related trained personnel. This simple need to sustain and expand their industrial quest, power, and wealth motivated the industrial titans like John D. Rockefeller, Andrew Carnegie, and others to donate a large sum of money and resources to these institutions so they could build infrastructure, improve the facilities, and maintain their sustainability. Also, these industrialists showed their benevolent nature and Christian teaching, which might have influenced numerous ex-slaves to convert to Christianity.

Industrialization of America created enormous wealth for industrialists and proved to be an effective way to uplift the economy, and to some extent, provide a better quality of life and comfort to the people. Vocational skills could be learned or mastered easily and these skill sets allowed people to earn a living that provided a sense of worthiness and social acceptance. These economic freedoms provided food and shelter and the basic necessities of life.

In the South many Black institutions opened their doors for the freed slaves so they could get an education. Once educational opportunities were available in the Black institution of higher education, numerous Black students enrolled in these institutions so they could be proud of their heritage and get an education that would help them earn a living and monetary security. This was an upward movement of Black youths toward higher attainment in academic sectors, which was only available to White race a few years earlier, created a fear in the minds of White communities that economic competition are looming soon. This fear of competition in the job market and attack/challenge on the supremacy of White race created a shockwave to the foundation of White Southerners. This fear of losing racial superiority over former slaves allowed upsurge of Ku Klux Klan and other racist organizations. Violence, rape, and lynching of young Blacks became the tool of oppression by these ruthless groups. The president of Talladega College was killed by the white gangs to show their power and these same people threatened the Black youths they should avoid educational institution to get an education. This intimidation and threat against education lasted for years in the South (Duster

2009). The ensuing economic competition and the fear of losing the supremacy triggered an avalanche of discord and hatred toward the Black race, which had been dormant for some time. The tension led to armed conflict among Blacks and Whites in 1870 (Duster 2009).

During this turbulent time, great educator and civic leader Booker T. Washington founded Tuskegee Institute in 1881. This institution built in the framework of creating public school teachers and an industrial labor force, concentrating on various trades like carpentry, ironsmith, and others. This educational philosophy (vocational) calmed the fears of Southern Whites about competition and allowed Washington to continue his educational enterprise. Washington used his intellectual genius and charisma to take the leadership of Black people and focus on building bridges between Northern and Southern Whites through cooperation and racial conciliation. Washington's simple but effective philosophy of education based on self-improvement and job training led to economic freedom, self-supporting craftsman, and industrial tradesman. This non-confrontational, conciliatory ideological manifesto made Southern White supremacists at ease and attracted Northern White philanthropists to fund the Tuskegee Institute. The Northern industrialists needed manpower to run their industrial empire, so they needed unlimited supplies of cheap, trained industrial workers that will maintain industrial productivity. By helping Black colleges and universities financially, the Northern industrialists assured the supply of cheap labor force trained in these Black institutions.

Washington was a leader who understood the political climate of America well. He observed that disputed national election of President Rutherford Hayes in 1876 that ended the Reconstruction era, and the political rights of Blacks. President Hayes' election helped the Democrats recapture the power and political control in the South. Southern democrats defied the federal government and instituted the segregation laws throughout the South, which required separation of Whites from "colored" on public transportation, the schools, restaurants, and other public places. The US Supreme Court in 1883 declared the Civil Rights Act of 1875 unconstitutional, and between 1890 and 1908, Southern states passed laws to disenfranchise Blacks (Taylor Jr. n.d.).

During this turbulent time, the Blacks lost all hopes of achieving freedom and dignity of their race. Washington understood the anti-black mood of the South, and he wanted to uplift the Black race toward the goal achieving freedom, equality, and justice. He knew the power structure in the country favored Whites, so the Blacks must not demand equal rights and justice, because they had no power to impose this on the White race. So he chose a softer pacifistic and conciliatory pathway to convince the Whites that Blacks would follow the leadership and political practices of Whites. By adopting this principle of political acquiescent, he won the support of Northern and Southern Whites to continue his activities of building up the Black educational process and creating a trained labor force that would support and maintain industrial, agricultural, and economic self-sufficiency.

As a polished statesman, Washington reminded the Whites, "Cast down your bucket among these people who have, without strikes and labor wars, tilled your fields, cleared your forests, build your railroads and cities, and brought forth treasures from the bowels of the earth, and helped make possible magnificent representation of the progress of the South." The intent of this reminder was to tell Whites that they should realize that progress, whether economic, cultural, or political, can be achieved only by the contribution of Blacks and Whites together as a team. He said, "In all things that are purely social we can be as separate as the fingers, yet one as the hand in all things essential to mutual progress" (Washington 1895).

Booker T. Washington knew real power needed education, economic solvency, and strength based on a gun. Unfortunately, his race did not have these resources at their disposal, so he built the essential ingredients to move forward toward attaining the ultimate freedom. He focused his attention on the most important requirements such as education and economic solvency. His ideas were revolutionary at the same time achievable within a short period. He emphasized vocational and industrial trade training for his people that could mobilize a large workforce within a short time, who were trained to do jobs that would control the agricultural and industrial productivity of this nation. Many people would achieve economical solvency that would raise their social status and improve their standard of living with a special bonus of better health and happiness.

This transformation gave the power to Black people so they were on equal footing with Whites and accepted as equal in course of time. Washington's grand scheme for Black Americans to achieve equality, dignity, civil rights, and educational attainments was a realistic, practical, and achievable goal.

Booker T. Washington believed his people could achieve respect and acceptance from Whites through economic self-sufficiency, self-assertiveness through financial prosperity, and hard work in practical trades, which are the essentials in society. Washington was a pragmatic and a shrewd politician who was far ahead in his visionary ideas than his White and Black peers. Industrial progress through technological advancement is the key for his people to secure a bright future and economic power for generations to come. Washington knew the power and brutality of the right wing groups like Ku Klux Klan, who used oppressive and violent means to silence the progress of Blacks in South. He used a method of pacifism and reconciliatory tone to subdue the White supremacist groups and developed a coalition of Whites and Blacks to prosper the life of African-Americans in America.

W.E.B. Du Bois was born in February 23, 1868, in Massachusetts. He was the first African-American who earned a PhD from Harvard University. He publicly opposed Booker T. Washington's "Atlanta compromise," an agreement that proclaimed/asserted that vocational education was more valuable to Black people than higher education, and downplayed the political aspirations of Blacks to be leaders and hold political offices. Du Bois criticized Washington for not demanding equality for African-Americans, as granted by the Fourteenth Amendment. He believed Washington's strategy was an inferior strategy and spearheaded a separate movement that demanded full and equal rights for the Black people.

Du Bois believed Black youths must get an education from institutions of higher learning, where students would follow rigorous academic curriculum including the classics, arts, and humanities, which would cause them to think critically and analytically. This rigorous academic preparation would allow these students to compete with students from other institutions of higher learning and prepare the future leaders of the nation.

Du Bois was an intellectual, and he believed his people could be free if their mind was sharp and they developed the skills that enhanced the intellect. He thought if schools could train students how to improve their thinking skills, they'd be thinkers and become the bearer of new knowledge, and creators of new ideas that would break the shackles of slavery and slave mentality forever. They would be the leaders and movers in the country. The White majority did not like the revolutionary ideas of Du Bois because they knew knowledge was the ultimate power. Emancipation and awakening the spirit of freedom was the final nail in the coffin of White supremacy and this demand the White majority did not want to relinquish, which triggered a violent response from Whites.

Du Bois's rhetoric about not submitting to humiliation, suffering racism, or losing manhood to achieve no changes and/or action by the majority of White people. Thirty years later Carter G. Woodson scoffed about the ideas of leadership, and said, "If the Negro could abandon leadership and instead stimulate a larger number of the race to take up definite tasks and sacrifice their time and energy in doing these things efficiently the race might accomplish something. The race needs workers, not leaders . . . when you hear a man talking, then, always inquire as to what he is doing or what he has done for humanity. Oratory and resolutions avail little" (Woodson; 1933,76).

Woodson believed Black scholars trained in universities in Northern and Western states did not understand about the matters that concern Black people. These universities provided various skill and scholarly pursuits in languages, sciences, and mathematics, which would serve nation well. But what students were taught in economics, history, literature, religion, and philosophy would not serve any Blacks any good, because information learned cannot be applied to the matter of concerns of Black people. This information might even misdirected (Woodson 1933, 2).

"The differentness of races, moreover, is no evidence of superiority or of inferiority. This merely indicates that each race has certain gifts which the others do not possess. It is by the development of these gifts that every race must justify its right to exist" (Woodson 1933, 5).

Ideological purity and practices do not put food on the table. They do not support the basic need of survival, but in the long run, persistence and desire to adherence can bring forth the changes where democracy would survive and flourish. Du Bois was a dreamer and purist to some extent, and a utopian philosopher, whereas Washington was a realist who knew freedom could be achieved in the long run if economic attainment was gained through non-threatening postures of the whole race. This way the White supremacists would relax their chokehold of cruelty on the Black people and Blacks could enjoy their life in peace with dignity.

CHAPTER 9

Legacies of Slavery

Part One

History acted as the silent witness of the traumatic, inhuman torture inflicted on the innocent African slaves by the American institution of slavery. It recorded each event of brutalized lynching, burning, rape, mutilation, murder, and destruction of the family by selling family members to various slave owners, through its own wide lenses for everyone to see. History is the chronicler who writes every event with no bias, manipulation, distortion, or any other lies. It records as things unfold in the bosom of time. If history was a human being, then it would shed tears flowing like mighty Mississippi River down the Southern Plains for centuries. White Americans destroyed Native American people so they could build their homestead and abused African slaves to develop their economic might and prosperity through the backbreaking hard labor by intimidation, torture, and beatings.

The institution of slavery and its brutal, violent, and inhumane treatment of African slaves caused unfathomable destructive impact on humans from severe trauma to toxic stress that passed along one generation to the next through the epigenetic modification of DNA structure. These problems created a myriad of different pathophysiological conditions that affected prenatal, postnatal, adolescence, adulthood, and old age throughout the whole life span of African-Americans for centuries.

All these negative experiences embedded within the African-American men, women, and children led to severe cases of mental disorders, PTSD, cognitive deficits, high death rates among newborn, malnutrition, rage, anger, and utter poverty.

Many families experience dysfunctionality responsible for all the antisocial behavior expressed by the younger generation of Black youths. They feel they are marginalized by society and undergo severe hopelessness and depression. High rate of incarceration, high school dropouts, a higher rate of pregnancy, violence, and the cycle of poverty are the legacies of slavery.

Many Whites do not understand effects of slavery could linger for centuries, and their ignorance and/or intentional naiveté point to the facts of the "underclass culture" that existed in our cities' ghettos. These Whites think that African-Americans and their Black culture perpetuate crime, despair, violence, and self-destructive behaviors (Loury 1998).

The Conservative Whites are vocal to point out that if Blacks "would get their acts together, like the poor Asian immigrants, then we would not have such horrific problems in our cities." But these Whites forgot the facts that their White forefathers created and nurtured slavery to extract every ounce of slave blood so they could get maximum labor output from poor Black slaves. These horrific practices created the toxic stress which through epigenetic modification of DNA structure caused all these debilitating diseases and mental disorders that reflected on the Black people's behavior.

To understand the scope and enormity of the impact of slavery, we have to know various parties, stages, and time frames of inflicting exposures responsible for various diseases that crippled the African-American mind, body, and spirit. For a better understanding of the legacy of slavery, we have to look at the various factors such as poverty, segregation, brutality, oppression, trauma, toxic stress, telomeres, and other environmental agents to create the legacies of slavery.

Poverty

Poverty is an offshoot of slavery in America. It is a phenomenon defined as when an individual does not have resources essential to meet the need for survival, such as money, food, clothing, and shelter, then the person is experiencing utter or absolute poverty. During the Second World War British scholar William Beveridge proposed that to confront the utter poverty the government should tackle "five giant evils" such as squalor, ignorance, want, idleness, and disease.

Five evils can be eliminated by improving housing, secondary education, income, employment, and health services (Reeves et al. 2016).

Poverty is a multidimensional entity. This multidimensional entity is influenced by low income/poor skills, poor health/poor accessibility to health service, insecurity, poor housing/neighborhood, poor education, risky behavior, high crime rate, and other negative factors that increase the levels of stress, and compounded the effects of poverty. If an individual does not have the skills to get a job, then he/she becomes poor, and then is forced to live in a housing area where insecurity, high crime rate, high risk of ill health, malnutrition, and other negative factors abound, the individual will live in abject poverty.

According to the US Census Bureau in 2015, 43.1 million people lived in poverty. The highest rates of poverty found among Black and Hispanic population (i.e., Black [24.1%], Hispanics [21.4%], Whites [9%], and Asian [11.4%]).

Destructive Influence of Poverty in Education

Poverty is the most destructive force against the educational attainment of children in the USA and it undermines the freedom of their existence. The US has the highest child poverty rates among all industrialized countries. This rate has an enormous impact on student performance and academic achievement. A large percentage of students drop out from the secondary schools for various reasons. One of the main reasons is the student's attitude and lack of self-belief that education can pull up these students from poverty and provide opportunities that will ensures economic stability and freedom. Poverty is a vicious cycle that is shackling the mind of young youths and a cultural doubt about their abilities that morphed into a medusa of hopelessness and meaningless existence. Poverty created an environmental cage that bound them within where crime, violence, and antisocial culture subsume them. Schools in this area usually have almost no access to resources essential for the nourishment of human mind, body, and brain.

The United States is the richest and most powerful country of the world, ranks second highest in child poverty among world's richest thirty-five countries (UNICEF Innocenti Research Center 2012). In the US among all children 22% are in poverty, whereas Black (28%) and Hispanic (25%) children are in poverty. These children live in households where parents have unstable employment (Coley and Baker 2013).

In 2011, according to official poverty criterion, 46.2 million Americans were in poverty, which represents 15 percent of the total population of US. Poverty among White Americans was 30.9 million (12.8%), 19.2 million non-Hispanic white (9.8%), 13.2 million Hispanic (25.3%), 10.9 million Black (27.6%), and 2 million Asian (12.3%) (Coley and Baker 2013).

Poverty is associated with many social problems and an important barrier for achieving academic attainment and upward mobility. The US Department of Health and Human Services yearly publishes a document known as Federal Poverty Level (FPL), a measure of income guidelines used to determine a person's eligibility for certain programs and benefits. This document delineates income levels to describe the poverty level. In 2016, if a person's income was below $11,800 dollars per year, he/she was living in poverty. If a family of four living in a house has a total income less than $24,300, then they will be eligible to receive various benefits such as Medicaid and Children's Health Insurance Program (CHIP) coverage, etc.

The public-school students are eligible for free or reduced price lunch (FRPL) under the National School Lunch program, if their family earnings meet the criteria of the Federal Poverty Level.

Children from families with incomes at or below 130 percent of the poverty level are eligible for reduced-price meals (US Department of Education n.d.). The percentage of school students eligible for free or reduced-price lunch provides a good indicator to measure the number of students coming from low-income family within a school.

High-poverty schools are defined as having over 75 percent students eligible for free or reduced-price lunch (FRPL) and mid-high poverty schools where 50.1–75.0 percent students are eligible for FRPL. Low-poverty schools where 25 percent less are eligible for FRPL, and mid-low poverty schools where 25.1 to 50.0 percent students are eligible for FRPL.

In 2012–13 school year, higher percentages of Asian students (38%), White students (29%), and students of two or more races (22%) attended low-poverty public schools than Pacific Islander (12%), American Indian/Alaska Nature (8%), Hispanic (8%), and Black (7%) students. High percentages of Black (45%), Hispanic (45%), and American Indian/Alaska Native (36%) students attended high-poverty public schools than did Pacific Islander students (26%), students of two or more races (17%), Asian Students (16%), and White students (8%) (US Department of Education n.d.).

The location of public schools is divided into four areas such as a city, suburb, and town or rural. Data from school year 2012–13 show that a majority (65%) of students attending city schools were in a high poverty or mid-high poverty schools, whereas a majority of students attending suburban schools were in low-poverty schools.

Impact of poverty on educational achievement and attainment

Studies on the impact of poverty on educational achievement and attainment revealed that two-year-olds showed 39 percent proficiency in listening comprehension among children are at or above poverty level. Children in poverty level showed proficiency in expressive vocabulary 55 percent, whereas children at or above poverty level achieved 67 percent proficiency level among two-year-olds (Coley and Baker 2013).

The early childhood longitudinal study in 2009 found four-year-old children in poverty achieved proficiency level of 20 percent in Letter Recognition, whereas four-year-olds at or above poverty level achieved 37 percent proficiency. Proficiency in Numbers and Shapes, four-year-olds achieved 45 percent who were in poverty, whereas 72 percent proficiency attained by children were at or above poverty level.

The data show that cognitive skills in listening comprehension and expressive vocabulary proficiency achievement varies between 10–12 percent among two-year-olds are in poverty and those who are at or above poverty level. But among four-year-olds are in poverty, proficiency achievement in Letter Recognition show 17 percent decline than children are at or above the poverty level. Cognitive skills in Number and Shapes show a 27 percent decline in proficiency level for children are in poverty. This dramatic decline in cognitive deficiency in analytical abilities among four-year-olds suggest that poverty is influencing the neurological development of children, which will have a long-lasting impact throughout their life span (Coley and Baker 2013).

Data from the National Assessment of Educational Progress (NAEP) in 2011 showed that fourth graders on average in reading scored 238 who were not eligible for free or reduced-price school lunch, whereas children eligible for a free lunch or eligible for a reduced price lunch scored 203 and 226. Among eighth graders the average reading scores were 279 for children not eligible for free lunch, whereas students eligible or eligible for a reduced price lunch scored 247 and 268 (NCES; Selected years 1992–2015).

Table 1. Average NAEP test scores in Reading in year 2011[15]

	Fourth Graders	Eighth Graders
Eligible for free lunch	203	247
Eligible for reduced lunch	226	268
Not eligible	238	279

National Assessment of Educational Progress (NAEP) data on reading proficiency among fourth graders eligible for free lunch showing that they are in poverty, scored 35 points lower than children who were not eligible for a free lunch., eighth graders eligible for free lunch scored 32 points lower than those children who were not eligible for a free lunch shown in Table 1.

College Board reported in 2012 that college-bound senior students with the lowest levels of family income scored about 100 points lower than those students' family income was at the top in SAT critical reading test (Coley and Baker 2013).

Poverty influences academic achievement. The international study of mathematics and science trends completed in 2007 showed that poverty negatively affects academic learning and retards the growth of intellectual development. Gonzales et al. (2008) observed that TIMSS scores went down if students representing the schools where 50% or more are in poverty. The US average score was 529 in TIMSS test, and international student average score was 500, the schools where 25% are in poverty, students score was 553, and schools with over 75% in poverty, the test score was 479.

The PISA (Program for International Student Assessment) test of 2009 revealed that fifteen-year-old American youths from US scored in reading an average 500, and the International Student average was 493 (Fleischman et al. 2010).

---

[15] NCES; selected years 1992-2015. The test scale score range (0–500). Retrieved from: https://nces.ed.gov/programs/digest/d16/tables/dt16_221.12.asp

The fifteen-year-old American youths attending a school where only 10 percent or fewer classmates from poor families scored 551 in PISA reading test, whereas students eligible for free or reduced price lunch (FRPL) program scored 446. Their reading scores are below, every participating countries in the Organization for Economic Co-operation and Development (OECD).

Condron (2011) showed through statistical modeling that if Finland, one of the highest-achieving nations in the world on PISA tests, has a childhood poverty rate of about 22 percent as in US, what would be the performance score in mathematics of fifteen-year-old test takers? The result from modeling experiment showed that math score will drop from a world-leading 548 to 487, which is below the international average score. US with a childhood poverty rate of 4 percent as with Finland, the PISA math score will rise to 509, which is above the international average score. This computer model strongly suggests that poverty plays a very crucial role in the educational achievement. Berliner; 2013, observed poverty and inequality affects student's academic performance.

Public and private schools are entrusted to prepare and train the pool of Nation's future workforce who are well prepared and equipped with the skills such as critical thinking, problem solving, and have the ability to transfer knowledge to solve future problems yet to surface in our globalized economy. The United States is facing a dropout crisis where over one million students of the 2012 graduating class will not receive their high school diplomas because of dropping out of schools for various reasons (Education Week 2012).

High school dropouts face a bleak economical, physical, and social prospects because they will earn low wages, live in poverty, and develop bad habits influencing health-related problems (Rumberger 2011, Rumberger; 2013).

Poverty is one of the main reasons for high school dropouts. It is responsible for numerous adverse conditions that are highly detrimental to the normal functioning of family well-being. Shonkoff et al. (2012), evaluated one of the major adverse conditions known as toxic stress and its lifelong effects on children's growth and development. Various factors can influence the human development process.

There is an intricate balance between the genetic predispositions and environmental influences that regulate development processes which will define the health and well-being of individuals throughout their life.

Research studies on student dropouts

School completion in the US in the recent times is around 90 percent (Baldwin et al. 1992, Chapman et al. 2010, Doll et al. 2013).

About 10 percent students do not complete their school education and drop out. High school completion is very important because it is customary to complete the high school and graduate. High school certificate or diplomas allow graduates to further their education in colleges and universities and also ensure a more stable job to support their families. The highest percent of high school dropouts are African-Americans, Hispanics, and other diverse groups.

High school dropouts create a tremendous economic burden on society, because most dropouts cannot get good jobs in this competitive globalized economy, and they have to be absorbed into social safety net programs such as Social Security, Medicaid, and food stamps. These dropouts cause economic pressure which increases poverty levels in the US.

It is important to analyze why these high school students drop out. According to Jordan et al. (1994), the students drop out from school because of pressure created by specific factors they coined as the "push" and "pull" factors. A student is pushed out of the school because of specific conditions like tests, poor social behavior, attendance, and discipline policies are violated. Specific agents influence the student such as economic worries, family needs, employment, and pregnancy.

Watt and Roessingh (1994) added another factor that also influences dropping out of school. Authors named this factor as "falling out" of school. This factor involves the individual's low efficacy toward academic attainment, and unwillingness to work to achieve the academic goals that leads to a condition of apathy toward continuing the academic pursuit.

The National Educational Longitudinal study (NELS: 88) revealed ranked reasons for a dropout in 1992 for tenth to twelfth grade students "falling out" of the school because they disliked the school by Hispanic (48%), Black (28.8%), and White (45.5%), and feelings that they do not belong to schools by Hispanic (16%), Black (25.9%) and White (26.6%) respectively (McMillen and Kaufman 1993, 36).

The "push" factor responsible for dropping out includes failing in the school, not keeping up with school work, unable to get along with teachers, or suspended/expelled from school. The "pull" factor involved job-related and family-related circumstances.

Table 2. Ten Ranked Reasons for a student to Dropout in 2006.[16]

Rank	Reason for Dropout	Males	Females
Push 1	Missed too many school days	44.1%	42.7%
Pull 2	Thought it would be easier to get GED	41.5%	39.1%
Push 3	Getting poor grades/Family school	40.1%	35.2%
Fall 4	Did not like the school	40.1%	32%
Push 5	Couldn't keep up with school work	29.7%	35.3%
Pull 6	Pregnancy	-	27.8%
Pull 7	Got a job	33.5%	20.3%
Push 8	Thought could not complete course requirement	22.9%	29.0%
Push 9	Could not get along with teachers	27.7%	21.6%
Pull 10	Could not work at their same time	23.1%	19.9%

---

[16] Selected Data from 2002 Education Longitudinal Study (Dalton et al. 2009). Dalton, B, Glennie, E., Ingels, S., and Wirt, J. 2009. Late high school dropouts: Characteristics, experiences, and changes across cohorts: A descriptive analysis report. Washington, DC: Institute of Educational Sciences. 22; Dropout Indicator 29, as cited in Doll et al., 2013.

High school administrators reported that "pull out" factors such as a job, pregnancy, supporting family, and "falling out" factors such as student apathy, unwilling to study, and low self-efficacy toward academic progress and achievement are the most important reasons for dropping out (Doll et al. 2013). Overall, the interplay between push, pull, and falling out factors control the high school dropout rate among students.

According to Pleis et al. (2010), high school dropouts age twenty-five and older experience poorer health conditions than individuals who completed the high school program and earned a diploma, regardless of income.

Stark and Noel (2015) reported the total dropout percentage of sixteen- through twenty-four-year-olds who are not enrolled in the high school and who lack a high school diploma or an alternate credential such as General Educational Development (GED) certificate in the country for male (7.3%) and female (5.9%) in the year 2012. The dropout percentage by race/ethnicity and sex in the year 2012 is shown in Table 3.

Table 3. High school dropout percentage by race/ethnicity and sex in the year 2012.[17]

Sex	Whites	Blacks	Hispanics	Asian/Pacific Islander	American Indian/Alaska Natives
Male	4.8	8.1	13.9	2.5	15.8
Female	3.8	7.0	11.3	4.0	13.5

---

[17] Data from Figure 3. U.S. Department of Commerce, Census Bureau, Current Population Survey (CPS), October 2012; (Stark & Noel, 2015). [Stark, P., and Noel, A.M. 2015. *Trends in high school dropout and completion rates in United States: 1972-2012 (NCES 2015-015)*. U.S. Department of Education. Washington, DC: National Center for Education Statistics, Retrieved 3/10//2018 from https://nces.ed.gov/pubs2015/2015015.pdf.

Levin and Belfield (2007) conducted a comparative analysis of economic impact between high school dropouts and high school completers/graduates, revealed that average dropouts costs economy 250,000 dollars over individuals a lifetime in terms of lower tax contributions, higher reliance on social welfare programs like Medicaid, Medicare, food stamps, and higher propensities for antisocial behaviors and activities.

The National Center for Education Statistics (NCES) presented a report on the national status dropout rates which measures the percentage of individuals in a given range who are not enrolled in the high school and have not earned a high school diploma or an alternate credential such as their General Educational Development (GED) certificate (NCES 2015-015).

According to this report in 2012, 2.6 million sixteen- through twenty-four-year-olds were not in school and had not earned a high school diploma and an acceptable credential such as a GED certificate. This data represented 6.6 percent dropouts out of a population of 39 million non-institutionalized, civilian sixteen- through twenty-four-year-olds living in US (NCES-2015). Females ages sixteen through twenty-four showed a lower dropout rate (5.9%) than males (7.3%). Dropouts rates for Asian/Pacific Islander students for ages sixteen through twenty-four (3.3%), Whites (4.3%), Black (7.5%), Hispanic (12.7%), and American Indians/Alaska Natives (14.6%).

Selected data (year 2007–2012) on the national status dropout rates among students aged sixteen through fourteen years showed a decline for all races/ethnic groups. Students realized that dropping out of high school is not an acceptable choice they should follow. This realization is because of social, economic, cultural, and family pressures that cause a positive influence to stay put in school and earn a diploma (Table 4).

Table 4. National dropout percentage rates for high school
student ages sixteen- through twenty-four-year-olds by sex
and race/ethnicity during the year 2007–2012.[18]

Year	Total	Male	Female	White	Black	Hispanic
2007	8.7	9.8	7.7	5.3	8.4	21.4
2008	8.0	8.5	7.5	4.8	9.9	18.3
2009	8.1	9.1	7.0	5.2	9.3	17.6
2010	7.4	8.5	6.3	5.1	8.0	15.1
2011	7.1	7.7	6.5	5.0	7.3	13.6
2012	6.6	7.3	5.9	4.3	7.5	12.7

Impact of dropouts on the economy and society

High school students who drop out from school for various
reasons negatively impact society. In particular, the dropout individuals suffer economic hardship that leads to life in poverty and
hopelessness. Persons aged eighteen through sixty-seven who did
not complete high school had a median income of 25,000 dollars in
2012, whereas persons who earned a high school diploma or alternate acceptable credential like a GED certificate had median income
of 46,000 dollars (Stark and Noel 2015).

According to Rouse (2007), over a person's lifetime, a person
who did not complete high school lost 670,000 dollars more than a
person who completed and earned a high school diploma.

Among adults in the labor force, a higher percentage of dropouts are unemployed or have difficulty getting employment, whereas
individuals who are high school graduates are employed (US
Department of Labor 2013).

---

[18] Institute of Education Sciences, National Center for Education Statistics
(NCES 2015-015), Table 8. Also, US Department of Commerce, Census
Bureau, Current Population Survey (CPS), October 1972-2012.

Part Two

Brutality and oppression

Bayou Boeuf Plantation owner Edwin Epps was a tyrant who was notoriously called "Negro breaker" for his sadistic and brutal treatment of slaves. He was a heavy drinker and often showed his drunken rage on the slaves. One day he stabbed his gentle slave Abram in the back for no reason at all, and his wife had to sew up the wound and saved the life of old Abram. Epps had a crush on Patsey who was the best cotton picker in the Bayou land. His wife knew it and she was so jealous about her husband's fantasy, she would ask other slaves to whip Patsey for no reason when Epps was not in the plantation. Patsy knew of this interplay between Epps and his wife, so she always stayed away from Epps (Northup 1853).

On a Sabbath day, Epps was looking for Patsey but she was not there in the plantation, then a few hours later Patsey came back in the plantation. Epps asked her where she went, she replied, "I went to see Harriet." Harriet was the wife of Mr. Shaw. Epps never liked Mr. Shaw because he fantasized that Mr. Shaw was having an affair with Patsey. His jealousy drove him in a rage that forced him to strip her naked and whip her with the rawhide so hard that flesh came out on each stroke. Blood, flesh, cries, and shrieks filled the air on that Sabbath day (Northup 1853).

In one of his visits to the South, famous architect Frederick Law Olmsted observed brutality committed by the plantation overseer, which he later described in his book. The overseer of the plantation was showing Olmsted different sectors of the plantation on horseback. While passing by a thicket bush, the overseer stopped his horse and asked who was there in the bush. A girl about eighteen came out and the overseer asked her why she was hiding in the bush rather than helping in the field. The girl said, "I was taking a break, because I was not feeling well." The overseer got off the horse, pulled the girl, and ordered her to take off her clothing and lie on the ground naked. Then he took his rawhide whip and struck her hard with it. She shrieked and begged for mercy. Each stroke of the whip peeled off the skin and flesh. Olmstead asked the overseer to stop whipping the girl. The overseer stopped lashing and then said, laughing, "If I hadn't punished her so hard, she would have done the same thing tomorrow. The next day half the people in the plantation would have followed her example . . . you northern people know nothing about it. They would never work at all if they were not afraid of being whipped" (Olmsted; 1860; Ladenburg, n.d.).

The white master or overseer of the plantation always used cruelty and torture for no reason, except to enjoy his sadistic pleasure out of these events. These Whites enjoyed stripping these girls to take away their womanhood but also the sexual fantasy of deflowering these women and raping them through the use of whips.

Lynching

The post-emancipation period provided ex-slaves the opportunity to mobilize their strength through the use of voting rights that strengthened their political power in the Southern states where ex-slaves population made up a majority. The Southern Whites realized that they were on the losing side of the political battle. Thus, they created an organization that used violence and intimidation to suppress the political gain made by the Black majority. The Ku Klux Klan, Red Shirt, and other White supremacist organizations used violence, including killing Black voters. During the Reconstruction era violence became a tool of choice to suppress and intimidate the black voters in the general election (Equal Justice Initiative; 2017).

From 1868 through 1871 an aggressive terror campaign by the Southern Whites killed over four hundred African-Americans to maintain the white supremacy in Southern states. Whites used lynching through mob violence under the pretext of administering justice without trial and torturing individuals to death who were marked as presumed offenders with no real proof of criminal activity or reason (Cardyn 2002, Equal Justice Initiative; 2017).

Whites fabricated charges of rape against Black men. This way "whites sought retribution for alleged rapes by targeting entire black communities with violence, public and sexualized attacks including forcing victims to strip, binding them in compromising positions, and whipping their genitals, widespread rape of black women, sometimes in front of their families, and genital mutilation and castration" (Trelease 1971).

Example of lynching

Nineteen-year-old and eight months pregnant woman named Mary Turner announced that her husband Hays Turner did not murder Hampton Smith, the plantation owner in Valdosta, Georgia. The mobs lynched Hayes Turner. Mary Turner said the perpetrator of her husband's lynching death would be reported to the county officials for justice. Her courage and defiance angered the locals and a mob of several hundred people dragged her to the Folsom Bridge over the Little River. The mob tied her ankles, strung her upside down, dowsed her clothes in gasoline and set her on fire. As she dangled from the rope and was still alive, a man ripped open her abdomen with a pocket knife. Her unborn baby slid out from the open abdomen and fell to the ground. The mob stomped and crushed the skull and killed the tiny baby with sadistic vengeance (Armstrong 2011, Bennett 1961, Ramos 2010).

In 1920 in Paris, Texas, the Arthur family lived at a farm as workers. Two brothers, Irving and Herman, were hardworking field workers, but the owner was abusive, so the brothers left the farm and found a job in the nearby town. The owner was angry because he did not want to lose the Arthur brothers, so he used a gun to threaten to kill them and alleged that two brothers were trying to kill him. The local White authorities arrested two brothers for breaking the peace and threatening a White man. These allegations circulated and White men were determined to lynch these two brothers so they could teach the whole Black community that Whites are supreme and Blacks must follow their demands.

On July 6, 1920, a mob of over three thousand men watched the lynching of the Arthur brothers. They tied them to a flag post at the fairground, tortured them savagely, and burned them alive. During the lynching the Arthur brothers' sisters were in jail under the pretense of protecting the girls from the mob, but the sisters were beaten and gang raped by over twenty White men while in police custody (Lynching in America).

Lation Scott was accused of "criminal assault" in Dyersburg, Tennessee, and subjected to lynching for his "crime" by the mobs. Thousands of White spectators gathered around a vacant lot near the courthouse. Leaders of the mob ripped off clothes and skin with knives. A hot poker iron was used to gouge out his eyes, and then they shoved the whole hot iron in his throat, and other body parts, before castrating him. Then they roasted him over for a fire for four hours. This inhumane torture on a human being conducted by the White mobs sent a message to the Black community that they are less than human and they must obey the White men's rule and orders. Not a single active member of the lynching mob was prosecuted for their criminal activities and got away with impunity (The Burning at Dyersburg, 1917).

Who were those mobs?
Poor Whites who worked in the field and other menial jobs treated by well-to-do Whites as useless White trash, scalawags, or swamp people. Poor Whites wanted respectability from their own race, but the rich and wealthy planters hated them. This scornful attitude from their White brethren raised anger and hatred among these White trash that resulted a brutal mental disposition for these people who became a part of the White mob involved in the process of lynching a Black man. The viciousness and cruelty that include prolonged torture, mutilation, and dismemberment and live burning of the victim provided a sadistic enjoyment for these angry and vicious lynching mobs. The White trash people believed that by joining the mob they could achieve some acceptance from their well-to-do White brethren and, perhaps, will be assimilated into their group. This desire to be a part of the upper-class White society by the poor White propelled them to be more jealous toward hardworking Black freedmen. Poor Whites labeled as "ignorant, illiterate and vicious" (Isenberg 2016, 180) by the White planters and industrial merchants. As poor Whites were not a part of the White society, they were furious toward Black men. Their anger and frustration made them more prone to violence that expressed itself during this carnival-like atmosphere.

Rape

Slavery's footprints of aggression and violence can be seen in the censuses of mulattoes. The mulatto population in America, particularly in South Atlantic and South-Central divisions during 1850 through 1890, provide a realistic evidence of sexual violence imposed on female slaves. All mulattoes were not the product of sexual violence, but a majority of them were. It is not possible to know the exact number where sexual violence was the culprit of this genetic signature, but the circumstances and environment of that era provide a reliable picture. US Census published slave schedules that described the black, mulatto, and colored population in the Continental United States beginning in the year 1850 and ending in 1890. The table inscribed below (Table 5.) focused on the mulatto populations in the South Atlantic division and South-Central division which comprised seventeen states: Delaware, Maryland, District of Columbia, Virginia, West Virginia, North Carolina, South Carolina, Georgia, Florida, Kentucky, Tennessee, Alabama, Mississippi, Louisiana, Arkansas, Oklahoma, and Texas.

Table 5. Mulatto population in South Atlantic and South Central Division of US during 1850 thru 1890.[19]

Year	Negro population	Mulatto population	Average percent Mulatto population
1850	3,352,198	384,162	11.46
1860	4,097,111	571,547	13.95
1870	4,420,811	557,464	12.61
1880	5,953,903	n/a	n/a
1890	6,741,941	1,100,285	16.32
1900	7,922,969	n/a	n/a

---

[19] Willcox, W.F. n.d. Data from Table 19, p.30. Retrieved from: https://www2.census.gov/prod2/decennial/documents/03322287no8ch1.pdf

Stress

Understanding stress and its biological impact

Stress is a biological and psychological phenomenon where a "reaction to a stimulus that disturbs our physical and mental equilibrium" (Psychology Today). Stress can also be defined as any uncomfortable "emotional experience accompanied by predictable biochemical, physiological, and behavioral changes" (Baum 1990). In other words, stress can be seen as a process that can start a change that might influence the homeostatic environment in any living system. This change can be positive or negative and real or perceived.

Stress with positive changes is essential for healthy living. It provides the energy, drive, and mental alertness that help people to overcome obstacles such as cognitive challenges, and complete their assignments/tasks on time. In contrast, if the persistent and negative changes of stress exert an overwhelming effect on the system, which can destroy/disrupt the homeostatic balance, then it can cause serious damage to the physical and mental health conditions.

The ability to cope with stress is controlled by a "set of interrelated brain circuits and hormone systems that are specifically designed to respond to environmental challenges" (National Scientific Council on the Developing Child 2005/2014, 2). The activation and restoration of homeostatic balance by a series of actions will negate or reduce the impact of stress called stress response.

Classification of stress

The National Scientific Council on the Developing Child has classified stress into three distinct types: positive, tolerable, and toxic based (National Scientific Council on the Developing Child 2005/2014).

Positive stress refers to a stimulus responsible for moderate elevation of stress hormones such as cortisol. It lasts for a short period and can cause brief increases in heart rate and blood pressure. This type of positive stress helps the child to develop a healthy stress response system to cope with day-to-day simple challenges a child would encounter in his/her life.

Tolerable stress responses are capable of creating a serious negative effect on the developing brain structure among children, but the effects are short-lived, which allows the brain to recover from transient damages imposed by the stress factors. This limited negative effect on the developing brain is reversible. Children with this condition need caring parents/adults who would provide a strong positive, loving, and supporting a role for this reversal process. This positive and optimistic environment would lower the impact of a traumatic experience such as death or serious illness (National Scientific Council on the Developing child 2005/2014). The positive and supportive adults provide the children protective scaffolding that allows them to absorb the impact of serious stressful events in their life as tolerable stress.

Toxic stress induces a strong, frequent lingering activation of the body's stress response system, which causes irreparable damage to the developing child. Chronic, stressful events such as child abuse or neglect, parental drug abuse, or maternal depression cause high levels of stress hormone in the developing child's body. These toxic stressful events are further amplified if the children have no caring adults' support to lessen the impact on them.

Some stressful experiences are essential for our physical well-being because these experiences allow us to cope with the situation that will guide us to develop our skills for growth, adaptation, and survival and allow us to expand our learning and resiliency. If the stressful experiences are chronic, long-lasting, and persistent, then behavioral, mental, neurological, physiological, and cognitive changes will alter the homeostatic balance of the human body and mind which will lead to various maladies including death (McEwen 1998).

Partners of stress response system

The regulatory role of the stress response system is carried by the brain through interconnecting neurobiological circuitry involving the limbic system and sympathetic adrenal medullary system. The limbic system is a group of subcortical structures and their connections involving hippocampus, amygdala, hypothalamus, and other structures are linked.

Amygdala is an almond-shaped region of the brain deep within the temporal lobe that associates with emotional processes such as anxiety, aggression, fear conditioning, emotional memory, and social cognition (Rajmohan and Mohandas 2007).

The hippocampus is a sea-horse-shaped structure in the inner region of the temporal lobe and based on architecture and connectivity. It is classified into four fields cornu ammonis (CA) 1–4 but CA4 is actually a separate structure and not an integral part of the cornu ammonis (Rajmohan and Mohandas 2007). In the hippocampus, there is another structure known as dentate gyrus, which is different from cornu ammonis fields, and it houses neuronal stem cells that can differentiate into neurons. The hippocampus plays a critical role in long-term, fact, and event-related declarative memory storage (La Bar and Cabeza; 2006).

The hypothalamus helps regulate body, temperature, hunger, thirst, and various emotional states. It controls the pituitary gland, which is the master gland that regulates various endocrine glands, and subsequent release of hormones into the circulatory system, which maintains homeostatic balance. The hypothalamus helps to coordinate the neural and hormonal responses to many internal stimuli and emotions (Raven et al. 2005).

The amygdala, hippocampus, and parts of the thalamus are the three brain structures that border the brain stem known as the limbic system. It can generate emotion and experience emotion through the interaction between amygdala, hippocampus, and the thalamus. The amygdala is the most important center for emotional memory (Reece et al. 2014).

The limbic structures of the fore brain play important roles in the regulation of hypothalamus-pituitary-adrenocortical (HPA) axis activities. The hippocampus regulates HPA axis activity by ending responses to stress (Jacobson and Sapolsky 1991, Herman et al. 2005). The stimulation of neurons from the amygdala activates the HPA axis that initiates synthesis and release of glucocorticoid into the systemic circulation (Matheson et al. 1971; Van de kar and Blair 1999). Stimulation of hippocampal neurons repressed activity of paraventricular nucleus (PVN) of the hypothalamus that inhibits glucocorticoid secretion (Rubin et al. 1966, Saplosky et al. 1966, Saphier and Feldman 1987).

Adrenal gland

Adrenal glands are located on top of each kidney. Each adrenal gland has two distinct parts. The outer part is the cortex, and the inner part is the medulla. Embryologically and functionally, these two regions are different. The cells of adrenal medulla have the same embryonic origin as neural tissue. These cells secrete hormones directly to the blood circulation and the adrenal medullary cells considered as neuroendocrine cells (Reece et al. 2014).

The adrenal cortex produces two groups of hormones: glucocorticoids and mineralocorticoids. Glucocorticoids released by adrenal cortex have two steroid hormones such as cortisol and corticosterone. The major role of cortisol is to regulate glucose metabolism and plays a major role in stress response system. Mineralocorticoids such as aldosterone play an important role in blood pressure and salt-water balance in the system and stress. The actions of cortisol and aldosterone are mediated through binding with intracellular receptors such as glucocorticoid receptor (GR) and mineralocorticoid receptor (MR) respectively (Bamberger et al. 1996).

Adrenal medulla

It is responsible for producing and secreting two hormones, epinephrine and norepinephrine, in response to stress. These hormones are synthesized from amino acid tyrosine and classified as catecholamines. Both these hormones play major roles in preparing the body to face actual or perceived life-threatening situations by mobilizing all physiological and psychological resources to cope with the threat and prepare the body system for fight-or-flight response.

Pituitary gland

This gland is known as the master gland in conjunction with the hypothalamus, controlling almost all parts of the endocrine system including the thyroid gland, adrenal glands, ovaries, and testes. The pituitary gland is located at the base of the hypothalamus of the brain. This gland has two distinct regions: the anterior lobe and posterior lobe. Functionally they act differently. Neurosecretory cells of the hypothalamus are extended to posterior pituitary gland via axons, which secrete neurohormones produced by the hypothalamic neurons (Reece et al. 2014). The posterior pituitary gland extends the hypothalamus and acts as a reservoir of the hormones such as vasopressin and oxytocin, and these are secreted by the neurosecretory cells of the hypothalamus and then transported via axons of the neurosecretory cells to the posterior pituitary gland. Nerve signals from the brain will trigger the release of these neuro-hormones to the blood stream.

Anterior pituitary gland

The anterior pituitary lobe produces many hormones, one of them known as Adrenocorticotrophic hormone (ACTH) which stimulates the adrenal gland to produce glucocorticoids such as cortisol during stressful experiences or situation. The hypothalamic neurosecretory cells synthesize and secrete corticotrophin releasing hormone (CRH) into capillaries. They then release them to another capillary system within the anterior pituitary lobe triggering the synthesis of ACTH of the endocrine cells of anterior pituitary gland. ACTH activates the adrenal cortex to synthesize and secrete cortisol, a glucocorticoid to regulate blood sugar metabolism in the system (Reece et al., 2014).

The cerebral cortex

The cerebral cortex has four parts or lobes: frontal lobe, parietal lobe, occipital lobe, and temporal lobe. Prefrontal cortex (PFC) is the anterior most region of the frontal lobe. It has extensive neural connections with amygdala, hypothalamus, hippocampus, and midbrain. The PFC expanded throughout the evolution of the brain structure, and in human prefrontal cortex is almost one-third of the total size of the cerebral cortex (Elston et al. 2006).

PFC plays a major role in executive functions where it initiates and executes new and goal-directed behaviors, planning, and active problem solving (Luria 1966, Denckla et al. 1994, Siddiqui et al. 2008). It has a significant role in encoding and retrieving memory such as episodic and source memory that involves learning through sequential memory (Fletcher et al. 1998, Stuss and Knight 2002). Verbal expression, development of ideas, and execution as well as the ability to use language and correct expression through proper speech is mediated by PFC (Drewe 1974).

Neural circuits of PFC have the ability to bring a conditional response to a traumatic event to its normal level, whereas amygdala will enhance a fear response when a traumatic event occurs. (Quirk and Mueller 2008). Amygdala increases the catecholamine release norepinephrine in PFC because of a psychological stressor, which impairs the function of PFC but enhances amygdala (Arnsten et al. 2015).

Stress response pathways (SAM and HPA)

Sympathetic-adrenal-medullary (SAM) system

An individual encountering a situation involving a threat, bodily harm, or a challenge can trigger a stress response that will activate the sympathetic nervous system, where sympathetic neurons release adrenaline and noradrenaline to the heart and other organs including the skeletal muscle system to energize and prepare the body for a fight-or-flight response.

The cells of the adrenal medulla act as modified postganglionic neurons because they have the similar embryonic origin as neurons and release hormones directly to the blood, instead of releasing neurotransmitters directly to the synapse. This modification is an essential adaptation that allows a burst of adrenaline to the blood so that whole body can be ready for the fight/flight response (McCorry 2007).

The total hormonal output of the adrenal medulla splits into epinephrine (80%) and norepinephrine (20%). Norepinephrine converts to epinephrine by an enzymatic reaction during the stress so that the body can receive the epinephrine immediately. Both epinephrine and norepinephrine increase the rate of glycogenolysis (breakdown of glycogen into glucose) in the liver and skeletal muscles, and release glucose in the blood's circulatory system so it's available to all cells of the body to produce energy (ATP) via oxidative phosphorylation.

Epinephrine and norepinephrine also increase heart rate, breathing rate, and dilate bronchioles in the lungs, which allow increase oxygen delivery to body cells. They also constrict blood vessels that supply blood to the skin, digestive organs, and kidneys so that more blood can be supplied to the heart, brain, and skeletal muscles during stressful conditions (Reece et al. 2014).

Epinephrine and norepinephrine are synthesized from amino acid tyrosine and they are grouped in the category of amine hormones, catecholamines. They are the fast-acting stress response pathway to tackle immediate life-threatening dangerous situations. In contrast, if the stress is chronic and persistent, then the body uses a separate mechanism to cope with the situation and involves the hypothalamus-pituitary-adrenal cortex (HPA) axis stress response system.

Hypothalamus-pituitary-adrenocortical (HPA) axis

The hypothalamus receives information from the environmental stimuli such as sight, sound, smell, temperature, or pain and interprets real or perceived danger/challenges to the body, which can alter the homeostatic balance, will trigger stress response system. The paraventricular nucleus (PVN) of the hypothalamus will release corticotrophin-releasing hormone (CRH), which then stimulates the adrenocorticotrophic hormone (ACTH) of the anterior pituitary gland. ACTH circulates in the bloodstream and activates the secretion of adrenal cortex to release adrenocorticoids, the cortisol that maintains a steady supply of glucose for energy.

Acute production of glucocorticoids from adrenal cortex enhanced the glucose metabolism, which provides energy to face a dangerous life-threatening situation, and prepare the body to fight-or-flee response (Padgett and Glaser 2003). Thus, the HPA axis and sympathetic-adrenal-medulla (SAM) work together to fend off the immediate threatening conditions. However, when the HPA axis activate persistently due to chronic, intense stress-related episodes, then the glucocorticoids can cause ill health and other maladies. The primary role of cortisol during prolong stress is to ensure the continued availability of glucose. This hormone promotes release of fatty acids from adipose tissue for use by the heart and muscle,

Glucocorticoids degrade contractile proteins in muscle cells so that amino acids from these degraded muscle to synthesize glucose. This induces loss of muscle mass. Also, it lowers immunity by suppressing immune and inflammatory responses for long-term stress response. Increasing glucocorticoid hormone production from adrenal cortex can activate the adrenal medulla to release catecholamine (Carrasco and Van de Kar 2003). Sympathetic nerves release norepinephrine.

Part Three

Early life stress (ELS)/Amygdala/Hippocampus

Exposure to early life stressful experiences such as maltreatment and poverty often compromises the development of children and leads to behavioral problems such as aggressive and oppositional behavior (Shonkoff and Phillips 2000). These problems at later times express themselves into various psycho-patho-physiological conditions (Belfer 2008, Reef et al. 2011).

Both amygdala and hippocampus are implicated as important players in socio-emotional activities and linked to the behavioral problems during dysfunctional conditions, particularly when exposed to early life stressful situations. The amygdala is responsible for emotional and social information processing, and damage to this area will lead to problems evaluating the significance of social stimuli (Hanson et al. 2015, Adolphs et al. 1995, Aggleton and Young 2000).

Research on animals using chronic immobilization stress (CIS) protocol revealed that enlargement of amygdala volumes (Mitra et al. 2015, Padival et al. 2013) because of increased dendritic arborization occurring in rats. Hyperactivity can also occur in the amygdala (Rosenkranz et al. 2010, Padival et al. 2013).

In humans, McEwen (2003) found that patterns of brain alterations take place during initial episodes of major depression, where larger volumes and increased functional activities occurred in amygdala (Fordl et al. 2003, Siegle et al. 2003). Sheline et al. (1998) reported that after repeated depressive episodes, amygdala volume decreased. Theoretical models proposed nonlinear effects of stress are responsible for nonlinear changes in the amygdala after early increased volume of amygdala through extensive dendritic arborization (McEwen 2005).

Enlargement of amygdala and hyperactivity might give away to eventual shrinkage of the amygdala because of apoptosis (Ding et al. 2010) or autism where increased amygdala volumes have occurred in early development, then small amygdala volumes are noted later in life (Schumann and Amaral 2005, Mosconi et al. 2009, Kim et al. 2010).

Smaller amygdalae structures are found in children exposed to various early life stressful experience such as physical abuse, early neglect, and low socioeconomic status (SES) (Hanson et al. 2015). Greater cumulative stress exposure is associated with smaller volumes in both the amygdala and the hippocampus (Hanson et al. 2015). Children who experienced physical abuse and came from low SES households had smaller hippocampal volume. Smaller volumes in amygdala and hippocampus as a result of ELS could be used as possible predictors of behavioral problems among people. Smaller volumes in amygdala because of ELS might lead to the possibility of developing long-term behavioral problems, whereas smaller volume of hippocampus might be a better predictor of greater behavioral problems in the future.

Maternal stress and low birth weight

Maternal stress during pregnancy can induce in poor coping behavior in childhood during adversity, aggressive and antisocial behavior, attention deficit and hyperactivity disorders (ADHD), and depression (Weinstock 2008). Severe emotionally disturbed children and adolescents have been found to have mothers who had experienced chronic prenatal stress during pregnancy when compared with mothers with emotionally stable children who had not experienced any stressful episodes during pregnancy (Ward 1991).

Research studies show that childhood environment and circumstances play a major role in whether adults and adolescents develop effective disorders (Buchanan et al. 2000, Goodman and Gotlieb 1999).Children with low birth weight have a higher risk of childhood behavioral problems (Breslau et al. 1988, Breslau 1995, Kelly et al. 2001, Weinstock 2001). All these studies suggest that gestational stress during fetal development may be more vulnerable to the physiological changes, which increases susceptibility of disease expression at a later date.

Intrauterine nutritional deficiencies during fetal development cause sensitivities to the hypothalamic–pituitary–adrenal (HPA) axis. Any alteration because of external insult such as stress can lead to low birth weight and increased cardiovascular diseases and diabetes (Phillips et al. 1998). Premature/low birth weight subjects have high glucocorticoid levels because of compromised HPA axis and experience increased vulnerability for developing depression and anxiety symptoms in response to early adversity during their life span (Patton et al. 2004).

Animal studies revealed exposure to various stresses during pregnancy cause lower birth weight offspring with elevated stress-induced glucocorticoid secretion and higher corticotrophin-releasing hormone activity (Weinstock 2001). Hack et al. (2002) reported that few men born with very low birth weight (VLBW) graduated from high school and enrolled in a post-secondary educational program because of low IQ and poor academic achievement.Lower rate of enrollment in four-year colleges among VLBW men shows that they cannot compete with their normal birth weight peers in educational and occupational achievement, which will translate to lower earning ability, poor social status, and poor upward mobility (Moss 1997).

Poor maternal nutrition during pregnancy such as iron deficiency and low vitamin D are associated with abnormal fetal development (Rodriguez-Bernal et al. 2012, Robinson et al. 2014). It also causes abnormal growth and development of the placenta, which can impair nutrient transfer to the fetus (Wu et al. 2012).

Health of the intrauterine environment can predict future health and disease of the fetus through the programming effect of maternal pregnancy nutritional condition. Low birth weight is an example of how nutritional condition regulates the fetal development and provides a picture of the intrauterine environment (Gluckman et al. 2010, Barker 1995).

Gluckman et al. (2010) advanced that the fetus should be developmentally plastic and capable of using various means to adapt itself within its entire uterine environment. This developmental plasticity is an evolved trait so it can accommodate various environmental conditions across the life course. The early fetal and neonatal development will experience various environmental challenges/stress that would induce greater physiological effect resulting alteration in developmental pathway. The fetal response to the stressful experiences does not create higher levels of adaptive ability (Lewis 2012, Lewis et al. 2014).

Telomere and stress

The tips of human DNA molecule comprise a stretch of 500 to 5000 repeated hexa-nucleotide sequence of 5'-(TTAGGG)-3' with a group of proteins form a protective cap at each end of the chromosome known as a telomere. Telomeres play important roles in protecting the chromosome from nucleases and preventing chromosomal end-to-end fusion (Karp, G. 2013). After each cell division, the telomeres of each chromosome end shorten. Because of this reason, the telomere length can measure the aging process of an individual and the telomere acts as a "mitotic clock" (Shalev et al. 2013, Karp 2013). Telomere end shortens each time the cells divide; this region can act as a recorder of various events in the lifetime of an individual and provides a unique window for us to see the changes that might have occurred. Telomere length is an important biomarker to assess the exposure of lifetime stress on humans (Epel, E.S. et al. 2004; Shalev, I. 2012; Geronimus et al. 2010).

In humans telomere repeat sequences can be 15,000–20,000 base pair (bp) long at birth, then extensive loss of the telomere region occurs during childhood and in adults the telomere length becomes 8,000–10,000 bp long.

The telomere five prime to three prime (5' to 3') strand is comprised of guanine-rich nucleotides known as G-strand and the complementary strand at the 5' end called C-strand because of cytosine-rich sequence. Three prime (3') ends of each chromosome have a single stranded overhang and no complementary strand in the telomere (Linger and Cech 1996).

Telomere DNA

Human telomere DNA sequence is presented in Figure 1.

5'- TTAGGGTTAGGGTTAGGGTTAGGGTTAGGG-3'
3'- AATCCCAATCCC-5'

Fig.1. Human telomere DNA sequence showing G-rich single strand 3'-end overhang

Three prime ends of each chromosomal overhang sequence interact with specific proteins to form a looped conformation that protects chromosomal DNA from nuclear digestion (Shammas 2011).

A single strand guanine-rich 3' overhang interacts with several DNA binding proteins and a "shelterin" complex that is comprised of six individual proteins like telomere repeat binding factor1 (TRF1), TRF2, repressor/activator protein1 (RAP1), TRF1-interacting protein2 (TIN2), TPP1, and protection of telomeres1 (POT1) (O'Sullivan and Karlseder 2010, Palm and de Lang 2008).

The shelterin complex and 3'-G-rich overhang of the telomere together comprise the protective cap that play a major role protecting the end of chromosome and maintain telomere length. Telomere length shortens 50 to 200 bp during each cell division (Huffman et al. 2000).

Telomere DNA sequence containing hexa-nucleotide repeat in human (TTAGGG) can bind with a specific DNA binding protein linked with the holoenzyme telomerase. This telomerase manages the addition of the telomere repeat, which will replenish the attrition of the sequences during each time a cell divides. Telomerase enzyme consist of telomerase reverse transcriptase (TERT), telomerase RNA domain that contains RNA template, and dyskerin (Cohen et al. 2007).

The RNA template region in the human telomerase comprises eleven nucleotides (3'-r CAAUCCCAAUC-5'), which recognizes existing telomere DNA repeat sequence, and encode the telomere repeat deoxy (GGTTAG) elongation in the 5'-to-3' direction (Gavory et al. 2002).

Telomere length shortens each time a cell undergoes cell division, and when it reaches a critical length, the cell stops dividing and reaches to a state called senescence (Shammas 2011). The reason to use the telomere length as the biological clock comes from the laboratory experiment. Laboratory experiments on human fibroblasts growing in the tissue culture revealed that cells can divide about sixty times before reaching replicative cell senescence. Human fibroblasts cells contain a low level of telomerase enzyme. Telomere length shortens each time cell divides then it reaches the critical length after sixty cell divisions, cells reaching the senescence stage. However, when fibroblasts are modified by inserting an active telomerase gene, telomere lengths are extended through telomerase activation, the fibroblasts cells continue to divide indefinitely confirming that telomere length as a biological "measuring stick" clock (Alberts et al. 2015). In adults, telomerase enzyme is expressed in male sperm cells, lymphocytes, and embryonic stem cells. Somatic cells rarely express telomerase.

Gender and telomere length

At birth telomere length is similar in boys and girls. However, by adulthood the length of telomeres are longer in female than men (Gardner et al. 2014). This gender gap between male and female telomere length in early adulthood may be due to a higher rate telomere attrition in men than women. In later adulthood, during menopause women have similar telomere attrition rate as men (Epel 2009). Women experience higher psychological stress (PS) than men (Cohen and Janicki-Deverts 2012).

Environment plays a major role in people's health because it includes various factors such as socioeconomic, neighborhoods, and sociocultural influences. Poverty is the direct cause of environmental detriment because it is responsible for many negative influences that dictate the total environment around people and expose the inhabitants with greater and wider stressors. Children with low socioeconomic status (SES) experience greater childhood infectious disease attacks and later become more susceptible to colds. Recurrent infections in childhood lead to higher T cell turnover might cause shorter telomere length (Cohen et al. 2004).

Role of stress on telomere

Telomeres are dynamic entity that can increase in length or decrease, due to various sociobiological signals emanating from environmental demands such as stressful conditions (Epel 2009). Telomere length (TL) changes slowly over time within a cell and it records all events over the life span of an individual (Epel 2009, Zeichner et al. 1999). Zeichner and colleagues reported that during infancy humans have 10,000 base pairs, which undergo rapid loss during childhood that ranges 30 to 60 base pairs a year.

Woman's nutritional status during pregnancy affects birth weight of the infant. Studies in rodents revealed poor inadequate nutritional regimen in pregnancy leads to low birth weight pups that have developed shorter telomeres in kidney tissue (Jennings et al. 1999) and aortic tissue (Tarry-Adkins et al. 2008) in early life.

Numerous studies reported that there is a strong link between chronic stress and poor health, increase risk for developing cardiovascular diseases and compromises immune functions (McEwen 1998). Cellular environment and stress such as oxidative stress involved in regulating telomere length and telomerase enzyme activity. In vitro studies showed that oxidative stress can shorten telomere length and antioxidant treatment can reverse the process of shortening telomeres showing that oxidative stress play important role in the telomere function (von Zglinicki, T. et al. 1995; von Zglinicki 2002).

According to Mathur et al. (2016), stress comprises three main components such as stressor exposure, perceived notion of stress, and physiological response to stress. Chronic stressor such as domestic abuse can trigger sustained physiological stress responses that affect the HPA axis to release cortisol which affect the telomere maintenance.

Recent reports show that cortisol exposure and individual cortisol reactivity, which are the central components of the physiological stress response system, cause shortening of telomeres (Haussmann and Heidinger 2015, Gotlieb et al. 2015, Tomiyama et al. 2012). Mathur and her colleagues (2016) theorize that an individual's current perceived stress can reflect sustained, high level stressor presence, which affects the psychological state of the individual and lead to chronic physiological stress arousal. This chronic stress arousal can influence the telomere maintenance and it can cause shortening of the telomere length.

Leukocyte telomere length (LTL) and lower telomerase enzyme activity observed among people experiencing perceived stress due to presence of chronic stressor such as parenting a child with a chronic condition (Epel et al. 2004).

Reduced telomere length was observed in leukocytes, myocardial and arterial wall tissue in cardiovascular disease (Chang and Harley 1995, Oh et al. 2003).

Cawthon et al. (2003) found that telomere length can be effective predictor of eventual mortality regardless of the cause of death.

Parks et al. (2009) reported in a large study involving over 647 sisters of women with breast cancer who experienced chronic perceived stress showed shorter telomere length in their chromosomes.

Following rape, many women develop mental health problems including increased risk for developing depression (Malan et al. 2011). They reported that in a cohort of sixty-four rape victims, nine rape victims were diagnosed with post-traumatic stress disorders (PSTD). This study found a significant association between leukocyte telomere length (LTL) shortening and PTSD showing that LTL might be an important marker for the risk to develop PTSD in women after experiencing traumatic events (Malan et al. 2011). Individuals with a history of childhood maltreatment such as physical and emotional neglect had shortened leukocyte telomere length when compared with individuals who had not experienced maltreatment during their childhood. This study suggests maltreatment might speed up cellular aging process (Tyrka et al. 2010).

Individuals diagnosed to have PTSD are prone to age-related diseases and have high mortality rate. Studies conducted by O'Donovan and colleagues (2011) found that individuals with PTSD exhibited a shorter LTL than a control group showing that chronic exposure to childhood trauma might have induced a higher risk for PTSD.

Telomere and educational attainment

Studies on healthy men and women aged fifty-three to seventy-six years from the Whitehall II epidemiological cohort revealed that individuals with lower educational attainment exhibited shorter leukocyte telomere length (LTL) than individuals who had higher educational attainment. These findings suggest a greater risk for rapid cellular aging among individuals who are socioeconomically compromised (Steptoe et al. 2011). Studies involving homogenous population of European women aged forty-one to eighty years found that lower educational attainment is associated with shorter leukocyte telomere length but not with the current socioeconomic status (Surtees et al. 2012).

Impact of slavery on African-Americans and legacies of slavery in America

DeGruy (2005) hypothesized that multi-generation trauma along with continued oppression and absence of opportunity available to people led to the post-traumatic slave syndrome (PTSS), and it is the causal factor for the development of "vacant esteem, ever-present anger, and racist socialization, which is responsible for the psychological damages that ingrained violent and abusive behaviors among many African American youths and adults" (121). She wrote "centuries of 'racist socialization' experiences where 'systematic and traumatic programming of inferiority' imposed on African Americans resulted in 'inferiority physically, emotionally, intellectually, and spiritually, thus rendering them completely ineffectual in their own eyes and the eyes of the surrounding society" (137).

DeGruy (2005) asserted that the slave experiences of African-Americans have a direct relationship on the current major social problems among African-Americans. Research on other groups who experienced oppression and trauma showed that survivor syndrome is pervasive in the second and third generation. The characteristics of survival syndrome include stress, aggression, and other psychosocial problems including interpersonal relationship skills. According to Danieli (1998), "viewed from a family system perspective, what happened in one generation will affect what happens in the older or younger generation, though the actual behavior may take a variety of forms. Within an intergenerational context, the trauma and its impact may be passed down as the family legacy even to children born after the trauma" (9).

DeGruy's thesis is based on sociological assumption, with no reference to the scientific evidence that supports the existence of post-traumatic slave syndrome (PTSS) responsible for all the social, psychological, and pathological behavioral expression in the African-American population passed down from one generation to the next. Oppression, torture, and other inhuman treatment can cause post-traumatic stress disorder (PTSD) in many people, but the percentage of affected people is less than 10 percent nationwide. The National Comorbidity Survey Replication (NCS-R) study using DSM-IV criteria estimated the lifetime prevalence PTSD among adult Americans to be 6.8% (Kessler et al. 2005). The lifetime prevalence of PTSD among men was 3.6% and among women was 9.7%.

According to the National Center for post-traumatic stress disorder, 60 percent of men and 50 percent of women experience at least one traumatic experience in their lives. Women are more likely to experience sexual assault and child sexual abuse, whereas men would experience physical assault, accidents, combat, and disaster or witness a death. People in the military have a greater chance of experiencing horrible and life-threatening situations that could lead to PTSD. Veterans of various wars such as Vietnam War, Gulf War, or Operation Iraqi Freedom (OIF) developed PTSD that ranged from 12 to 15 percent. The National Vietnam Veterans Readjustment Study (NVVRS) estimated about 30 percent Vietnam veterans have had PTSD in their lifetime (National Center for PTSD; n.d.).

From post-traumatic stress disorder (PTSD) data, it is evident that "posttraumatic slave syndrome (PTSS)" alone could not be responsible for the large number of African-Americans who were the victims of injustice, inequality, and other sociocultural, economic disparity existing today in America.

The institution of slavery made African slaves a sub-human commodity. They experienced torture, lynching, rape, whipping, mutilation, extreme hard labor, and poor housing and living conditions that created total oppression, lifelong agony, and fearful existence. All these experiences led to a life with chronic toxic stress and trauma that resulted in acute poverty, a deficit in executive cognitive function, cognitive learning disabilities, neurobehavioral and mental disorders, depression, post-traumatic stress disorders, poor health developmental disabilities, autism, mood swings, high vigilance, a higher death rate in children, and a myriad of maladies, particularly cardiovascular abnormalities and metabolic diseases.

This chronic toxic stressful existence and abuse triggered epigenetic modification of DNA via methylation/demethylation, histone acetylation/deacetylation, and other processes that caused psychosocial, neurobehavioral, cognitive deficiencies and increased susceptibilities to physiological alteration leading to diseases. These conditions were often passed along from one generation to the next.

That was the legacy of slavery and the root cause of negative characteristics that dominated the whole history of Black people in America. This toxic stress syndrome (TSS) runs deep in the veins of African-Americans and prevents them from achieving excellence and full potential in all facets of life.

Slavery in America left an indelible scar and guilt on the psyche of White Americans. African-Americans were burdened with a history of abuse, trauma, and violence that translated into hopelessness, despair, and poverty. Sexual violence on women by Whites were very common practices during those years of darkness in the history of American Republic. The institution of slavery mocked democratic idealism based on human equality and justice for all. Many Americans believe those dark years of past must be forgotten and left behind so that the new day can bring a better prosperous life for all can be attained in America. Unfortunately, the legacy of slavery cannot be erased because the fruits of slavery are embedded in the heart of the society, and every day it is raising its head to warn us that we as a nation are faltering in our desire to fix the monstrous inequality and injustice that is engulfing our nation. We are dragging it down to the bottom of our existence as a republic.

CHAPTER 10

Epigenetics

Epigenetics: Definition

Waddington (1942) coined the terminology epigenetics to describe "the branch of biology which studies the casual interactions between genes and their products, which bring the phenotype into being." The concept of epigenetics in a broader sense describes the connection that bridges the genotype that expresses into the final outcome, without affecting the actual DNA sequence. Cells of multicellular organisms have identical genotypes, but during development generate a multitude of diverse types of cells that differentiate into cells with different biological functions. For this reason, cellular differentiation may be considered as an epigenetic phenomenon because changes occur without any alterations in genetic inheritance (Goldberg et al. 2007).

Goldberg et al. (2007) proposed a new definition of epigenetics that states "it may be defined as the study of any potentially stable and, ideally, heritable change in gene expression or cellular phenotype that occurs without changes in Watson-Crick base-pairing of DNA." The term *epigenetics* is used to describe any process that can induce changes or alteration in the gene activities without causing changes in the actual DNA sequence. This epigenetic process can be transmitted across generations from one generation to the next via cell division.

Foundational Evidence for Epigenetics

Development of defensive response to threat in mammals is regulated by the maternal care, particularly in rodents. Maternal behavior serves as the basis for the transmission of stress responses from mother to offspring (Weaver et al. 2004, Levine 1994, Fleming et al. 1999, Meany 2001).

Mother-pup contact in rats begins after birth during the first week of life, when the mother approaches the pups, licks, grooms, and nurses it. There are two forms of maternal behavior: the licking-grooming (LG) and arched-back nursing (ABN), which influences the development of individual differences among pups in behavior and HPA-axis response to stress.

The maternal influences the development of defensive responses to threat among its offspring through increased HPA activity. This helps them cope with the day-to-day stressful experiences. How can this maternal influence be transmitted across generations? Weaver et al. (2004) provided some intriguing answers that suggest strongly that "experience of the mother is translated though an epigenetic mechanism of inheritance into phenotypic variation in the offspring. Thus, maternal effects could result in the transmission of adaptive responses across generation" (Agrawal 2001, Rossiter 1999, Meaney 2001).

Four major levels of epigenetic changes have been identified: (1) chemical modification of DNA nucleotide base pairs such as covalent addition of methyl group as well as demethylation, (2) post-translational modification of histone proteins via methylation and acetylation, (3) modification by RNA interference (RNAi), and (4) nucleosome remodeling (Graff et al. 2011).

DNA Methylation

5-methyl cytosine (5mC) is a modified Cytosine that has been methylated with the addition of a methyl (CH_3) group via covalent attachment by the enzyme DNA methyltransferase (DNMT) found entirely within CpG dinucleotides (i.e., CpG refers to nucleotides of

C and G in DNA that are connected by a phosphodiester linkage). The methyl group donor is S-adenosylmethionine (SAM).

Most CpG sites outside the regulatory regions are methylated extensively whereas in gene promoter and enhancer areas are methylated less, indicating that CpG sites in the promoter region can be available for methylation, which will allow regulating the gene expression effectively. Most cases indicate that DNA methylation is an effective way to repress transcriptional activities and gene silencing (Goll and Bestor 2005).

In most cases, the DNA methylation in the promoter region suppresses the transcriptional activities because methylation blocks the binding with the transcription factors directly or recruiting the methyl-CpG binding proteins (MBPs), which repress chromatin-remodeling activities (Graff et al. 2011). Approximately 70–80 percent of cytosines in CpG dyads are methylated on both strands of DNA in human somatic cells (Chen and Riggs 2011). Sometimes, only one of the strands of DNA cytosines is methylated, then it is called hemi-methylation.

There are three active DNA methyltransferases (DNMTs) present in mammals: DNMT1, DNMT3A, and DNMT3B. The enzyme DNMT1 is believed to function as a major maintenance enzyme for methylation duties and it has a preference for hemi-methylated CpG sites generated during DNA replication (Pradhan et al. 1999) and is "responsible for copying the pre-existing methylation pattern to newly synthesized strand" (Chen and Li 2004).

One of the best evidences in support of the role of DNA methylation regulating actively post-mitotic cells came from the work on rodents. Weaver and Colleagues (2004) showed that quality of maternal care received by the pups during the first postnatal weeks was directly influenced by the DNA methylation patterns of the glucocorticoid receptor gene (GR) in the pups and maintained throughout the life span of these animals.

To determine if maternal care can change the DNA methylation pattern of specific target site of the GR promoter in rat, Weaver and Colleagues (2004) mapped differences in the methylation status of individual cytosines within the CpG island of the exon I-7 promoter from hippocampal tissues obtained from adult offspring of high and low-LG-ABN mothers. Cross-fostering analysis revealed that in the low-LG-ABN offspring fostered by high-LG-ABN dams, methylation pattern within the exon I-7 promoter was "indistinguishable from biological offspring of high-LG-ABN mothers." Similarly, methylation pattern offspring from high-LG-ABN mothers reared by low-LG- ABN dams were comparable to that of low-LG-ABN offspring. These findings support the notion that "variations in maternal care directly alter the methylation pattern of the exon I-7 promoter of the GR gene, and provide an explanation for the enduring effect on mother-infant interactions over the first week of postnatal life on HPA responses to stress in the offspring" (Weaver et al. 2004).

As adults, offspring of "high-LG-ABN" mothers exhibit low HPA-response to stress and less fearful responses than offspring of "low-LG-ABN" mothers (Stern 1997, Liu et al. 1997, Caldji et al. 1998, Francis et al. 1999).

Epigenetics/Gene Suppression

In most cases, DNA methylation causes suppression of gene activity via negative regulation of gene transcription. DNA methyltransferases (DNMTs) transfer methyl groups to cytosine residues at the 5-position of the pyrimidine ring of CpG dinucleotide occurring in small clusters commonly known as CpG islands (Miranda and Jones 2007). These CpG sequences are present near the promoter region of genes.

Once specific CpG dinucleotide cluster sequences are methylated, they trigger the enlistment of the transcriptional suppressors such as methyl CpG-binding protein2 (Me CP_2) histone deacetylase (HDACs) and chromatin remodeling co-repressor creating a three-dimensional DNA-histone protein complex that induces condensation of the chromatin structure. This condensed chromatin complex blocks the transcription machinery and subsequent suppression of transcription process (Roth et al. 2010, Miranda and Jones 2007).

Versatility of DNA Methylation Process

Embryonic development

Normal embryonic development is dependent on the DNA methylation process, and it plays an important role in gene regulation and expression. Studies revealed that during mouse development process, methylation, and demethylation levels change and are under strict regulatory control. The fertilized egg undergoes demethylation during the preimplantation stage, where the same inherited parental methylation patterns are erased. After implantation, extensive de novo methylation occurs, which creates new methylation pattern in the developing embryo (Monk et al. 1987, Howlett and Reik 1991). Paternal demethylation may allow reprograming paternal germline imprints by the maternally produced oocyte cytoplasm (Reik and Walter 2001).

Many genes that are responsible for imprinting where permanent gene silencing occurs are highly methylated. Imprinting is a process where one of the two alleles of a gene pair is silenced via epigenetic means such as methylation as well as acetylation (Weinhold 2006).

DNMT 3A and DNMT 3B are responsible for de novo methylation process on non- methylated DNA during early development (Okano et al. 1999).

The state of chromatin activity is regulated by the DNA methylation, and chromatin dynamics play an important role for the access of promoters by various transcription factors (Kadonaga 1998, Razin 1998). The maternal effect on DNA methylation resulted in significant increase in acetylation at residue K_9 of histone H_3 of exon I_7 GR promoter in the adult offspring of high-LG-ABN mothers compared with adult offspring of low-LG-ABN mothers. These findings strongly support the hypothesis that "DNA methylation pattern can be established through a behavioral mode of programing without germline transmission" (Weaver et al. 2004).

Cytosines of CpG island in DNA, when methylated, it attracts DNA-binding proteins and histone deacetylase (HDAC) which remove acetyl groups from lysine residues of histone proteins thus blocking the acetylation process and promote the binding of transcription factors (Roth et al. 2001, Cervoni and Szyf 2001).

Timing of the maternal effect on DNA methylation

The maternal care of high and low LG-ABN mothers differ only during the first week of life (Liu et al. 1997, Caldji et al. 1998). The significant differences in the methylation pattern between the two groups (high and low LG-ABN dams) occurred during post-natal day 1 (P1) and day 6 (P6) in the exon I_7 GR promoter. It is interesting to note that just before birth (embryonic day 20, E20), the entire region un-methylated in both groups (Weaver et al. 2004). Studies suggest the group difference in DNA methylation pattern can be found only during the first week of life, indicating that maternal behavior expressed during the first week after birth will program the offspring for life and this first week of postnatal life is the most critical period for the effects of early experiences on hippocampal GR expression (Meaney et al. 1996, Weaver et al. 2004).

Influence of Stress on Epigenetic Regulation

Maltreatment/methylation of DNA

Infant rats exposed to maltreatment by a caregiver induces hyper-methylation of brain-derived neurotrophic factor (BDNF) DNA in the prefrontal cortex, and the effects persist throughout the life span through reduced BDNF gene expression (Roth et al. 2009). Lasting changes in DNA demethylation of the arginine vasopressin (AVP) gene in the paraventricular nucleus has been found due to maternal separation stress experienced by the offspring (Murgatroyd et al. 2009).

Epigenetic control of memory formation via DNA methylation

Within twenty-four hours of the contextual-fear conditioning, the hippocampal changes in DNA methylation have been erased. These findings suggest DNA methylation and demethylation changes due to contextual-fear conditioning are supporting memory formation for a short period of time rather than long-term storage in the hippocampus (Miller and Sweatt 2007, Lubin et al. 2008).

LTP/DNA methylation
Laboratory studies found that demethylation agents zebularine and 5-aza-2-deoxycytidine treatment show alteration in DNA methylation pattern of the BDNF (brain-derived neurotrophic factor) and reelin (RELN) genes in hippocampal tissue as well as disrupts LTP (long term potentiation) induction (Levenson et al. 2006, Miller et al. 2008).

Adverse childhood experiences (ACEs)
Labonte' (2012) reported that increased DNA methylation of the glucocorticoid receptors in the hippocampus among suicide completers who were abused during their childhood indicating a strong link between ACE and epigenetic modification of the HPA axis regulatory mechanism. This report provided additional support to the findings of McGowan et al. (2009) that showed greater methylation levels in the CpG sites of the promoter region in the exon 1F of the glucocorticoid receptor gene among the suicide completers who experienced childhood abuse and trauma during their early-life development (McGowan et al. 2009).

FKBP5 gene is an essential regulator of the stress response system that showed a reduced methylation levels among children who experienced abuse during their childhood (Klengel et al. 2013). This reduction in methylation pattern shows an influence in cognitive abilities of these children indicating FKBP5 may have a regulatory role in cognition.

Histone structure

Chromosomes are composed of DNA and basic proteins commonly called histones and together form a complex called chromatin. Roger Kornberg in 1974 proposed a new structure for chromatin that comprised of repeating structure as nucleosome. Nucleosome core particle is made up of supercoiled DNA consist of 146 nucleotide base pairs wrapped around eight core histone molecules.

Chromatin that remains compacted during interphase is called heterochromatin, whereas euchromatin is a dispersed active state. Heterochromatin is divided into two classes: constitutive and facultative chromatin (Karp 2013). Constitutive chromatin remains in the compacted state in all cells, and this represents that DNA is permanently silenced. In mammalian cells, constitutive heterochromatin is found in regions close to telomere and centromere of each chromosome, and it is also located in the distal arm of Y chromosome of male mammals. These regions contain primarily repeated sequences and with very few genes. Facultative heterochromatin specifically inactivated during certain stages or in certain types of differentiated cells. The cells of male has tiny Y chromosome and a much larger X chromosome, whereas female cells have two X chromosomes, only one of them is transcriptionally active, and the other X chromosome remains compacted as Barr body, which is inactive (Karp 2013).

Eight histone molecules are organized into four heterodimers-two H2A/H2B dimers and two H3/H4 dimers. C-terminal domains play a key role for the dimerization of the histone molecules due to the presence of large numbers of α-helices which fold to form a compact mass in the core particle of the nucleosome. The N-terminal portion of the histone molecules form a "tail" that stick out of the DNA wrapped around the core particle (Karp 2013).

Histones are small proteins and their mass ranges from 11.0 to 23.0 kDa and possess usually large number of basic amino acids such as lysine and arginine. Histones are divided into five classes such as H1, H2A, H2B, H3, and H4. Histone H1 has the highest mass of 23.0 kDa in calf thymus and contain 215 amino acid residues. The H1 histone molecule act as a "linker because it binds to part of the

linker DNA that connects one nucleosome core particle to the next"
(Karp 2013).

The amino terminal (N-terminal) tail of the histone proteins
that stick out of the super coil DNA in the nucleosomes can be
enzymatically modified via the addition of various functional groups
through covalent linkages such as methyl, acetyl, and phosphate
groups. Basic amino acids residues such as lysine (K) and arginine
(R) can be methylated by the addition of methyl groups by the
enzyme histone methyltransferase. Similarly, lysine can be acetylated
by covalent addition of acetyl group through the enzyme histone
acetyltransferases (HATs). Serine (S) residues can be phosphorylated
by the addition of phosphate groups (Karp 2013, Allis et al. 2007).

Histone code and histone modification

Nucleosome with histone tails projecting outward model provides a very interesting way to achieve histone modification through
the enzymatic addition or removal of active groups that can act as
switching mechanism for gene activation or suppression. Lysine and
arginine residues of histone tail can be methylated, acetylated, phosphorylated, or ubiquitinated.

Histone H3 lysine at N-terminal position 9 (H3K9) can be
acetylated by the covalent addition of acetyl group through enzymatic process by histone acetyltransferases (HATs). This acetylation
of histone tail neutralizes the positive charges of histone and disrupts the binding to the negatively charged DNA which resulted a
site-specific loosening that promotes a transcription factor bindings
(Kadonaga 1998, Roth et al. 2001).

Modified histones develop stronger affinity for regulatory proteins and impact the expression of transcriptional activities positively
or negatively. For example, in most cases acetylation of lysine residues
lead to the activation of the transcription. The effects of methylation
can lead to activation or suppression of gene transcription depending
upon the location and amino acid residues modified.

Histone H3 protein is made up of 135 amino acids and the
amino acid sequence has been identified. The amino acid sequence
revealed that lysine (K) are located at position number 4, 9, 14, 18,

23, 27, 36, 37, and 79 respectively. All of these lysine sites are capable of methylation. For example, methylation of lysine 9 of histone H3 (i.e., H3 K9), lysine 27 (H3K27) of H3, and lysine 20 of H4 (i.e., H4K20), all strongly repress the transcriptional activities. In contrast, methylation of lysine 4 and 36 of histone H3 (i.e., H3K4me and H3K36me) is associated with transcriptional activation (Allis et al. 2007, Karp 2013). Similarly, there are other catalytic enzymes present that can specifically remove active groups such as acetyl, methyl, and phosphate groups from the histone tail.

During brain development histone acetylation process is important because specific sites on the chromatin that are acetylated/de-acetylated in conjunction with transcription factor can form complexes that can act as regulatory switches to activate or deactivate the gene expression pathway. Similarly, methylation at specific site controls the transcription process. Addition of three methyl group on lysine 27 on histone 3 (H3K27me3) has been found to be a transcriptional restrictor on promoters and play a major role in X-inactivation (Schoeftner et al. 2006). Trimethylation of lysine 9 on Histone 3 (H3K9me3) modification cause transcription silencing.

Epigenetic control of memory formation via histone modification
Mice that were exposed to contextual conditioning and learned contextual fear association showed significant increases in both acetylation and phosphorylation of H3-histone protein (Levenson et al. 2004, Chwang et al. 2006). Similarly, histone deacetylase (HDAC) inhibitors also enhanced memory in these animals (Levenson 2004). These results strongly suggest that histone tail epigenetic modifications influence long-term memory capacity (Roth et al. 2010).

Cognitively impaired mice treated with sodium butyrate, an inhibitor for histone deacetylase enzyme (HDAC), restored learning and memory function (Fischer et al. 2007). Similarly, Miller et al. (2008) reported that DNA methylation and histone acetylation work together to regulate memory formation.

RNA interference (RNAi)

Single-stranded interfering RNAs(RNAi) are produced from double-stranded RNA (ds RNA) and these single-stranded RNAs are short, usually 20–30 nucleotides long, selectively bind with complementary base paring and capable of inhibiting the process of translation as well as catalyzing the destruction of the mRNA (Alberts et al. 2015).

There are three different classes of small noncoding RNAs that have been found such as micro RNAs (miRNAs), small interfering RNAs (siRNAs), and piwi-interacting RNAs (piRNAs). The microRNAs regulate a large number of human protein-coding genes. The miRNA precursors are synthesized by the RNA polymerase II and mature miRNAs typically 23 nucleotide in length and assembled with a group of proteins forming a structure commonly called RNA-induced silencing complex (RISC). This complex is capable of targeting mRNAs with complementary nucleotides sequence with the help of Argonaut protein. Once miRNA is perfectly paired with mRNA, the RISC does not slice the mRNA in humans, instead the translation of mRNA is repressed and subsequently degraded (Alberts et al. 2015). In this way the miRNAs regulate the gene expression. In humans a single miRNA can regulate a large number of different mRNAs (Alberts et al. 2015, Hutvagner et al. 2001).

Several studies reported stress exposure can cause changes in microRNAs (miRNAs) expression in brain (Meerson et al. 2010, Rinaldi et al. 2010, Uchida et al. 2008). MicroRNA (miRNA) expression is associated with various psychiatric disorders including anxiety and depression (Dias et al. 2014b, Issler and Chen 2015). Volk et al. (2016) showed microRNA-15a (miR-15a) play a critical role in coping with the behavioral responses because of chronic exposure of stressful events such as childhood trauma.

MicroRNAs comprise two subgroups. One regulates epigenetic pathway-related enzymes such as DNA methyltransferases (DNMTs) and histone deacetylases (HDACs), which control transcriptional machinery, whereas other subset of miRNAs control gene expression post-transcriptionally. It appears that miRNA-epigenetics regulatory circuit controls the whole gene expression system (Sato et al. 2011).

Any disruption of this regulatory circuit will alter the physiological homeostasis and lead to various diseases.

Legacies of slavery left an indelible scar on the psyche of African-Americans. The people suffered abuse, trauma, sexual violence, lynching, dehumanization, mutilation, castration, segregation, and chronic toxic stress exposure throughout their life span from one generation to the next for centuries. The African-American's existence is burdened with abuse and toxic stress that triggered changes through chemical modification of DNA nucleotide base pairs via covalent addition of methyl groups, post-translational modification of histone proteins by methylation and acetylation, disruption of miRNA-epigenetic regulatory circuit that cause dysregulation of gene expression system, and other processes. All these epigenetic changes led to psychosocial, neurobehavioral, cognitive deficiencies and increased susceptibilities to physiological alteration leading to diseases, some of them lasting for more than one generation.

CHAPTER 11

Anatomy of Private Historically Black Colleges and Universities (HBCUs)

Historically Black Colleges and Universities (HBCUs) in America are unique academic institutions. They were created during the period of slavery and post-slavery era. The private HBCUs developed their own way to operate these institutions and many do not follow the normal operating procedures delineated by other academic institutions. To understand how these private HBCUs operate, the following passage describes its modus operandi.

The mission of the Association of Governing Boards of Universities and Colleges (AGB) is to "strengthen and protect this country's unique form of institutional governance through its research, services, and advocacy." This national organization serves over 1900 institutions and provides resources that enhance their effectiveness. AGB conducted a survey of Historically Black Colleges and University (HBCUs) presidents to seek their opinions regarding the strategic issues involving their own institution and the HBCU communities (AGB Report; n.d.).

The survey was sent to ninety-nine HBCUs presidents electronically. Only twenty-four responses were received (24%), of which 54 percent responses were from private institutions, and 45 percent from public institutions. Seventy-six percent (76%) HBCUs presidents felt that the survey instrument was not important for their institutional priorities they ignored the survey request. These types of attitude reflect the mentality of many HBCUs presidents they need no help or suggestions from another academic organization to improve their strategic operational policies that will ensure sustainability, academic quality, and preserve institutional mission.

The majority of private HBCU institutions guard their operational policies and they are not at all willing to share their ideas with other organizations. They feel that if they share their operational policies, then they will expose their mismanagement or unacceptable operational procedure that violates normal functioning of the business model they're using for the institution.

What is governance?

The effective operation of the academic institution depends on how the institution is governed. The governance of an institution is rested on three pillars the role of the board of trustees, the president, and faculty senate/association. All these three components must work together and share responsibilities to ensure that the goals and mission of the institution is preserved and create a sustainable financial foundation that enhances academic excellence now and into the future. Shared governance in academia must follow a system where various parties agree on issues of institutional direction based on the understanding of the challenges facing the institution. They should make correct decisions regarding operational issues such as academic programs, budgeting, student recruitment and retention, student activities, promotion-tenure policies (Bahls 2015).

Three pillars of governance must work in unison to create a holistic, cordial environment and transparency that ensure successful preservation of the institutional mission, academic excellence, and institutional existence.

Role of board of trustees

Board of trustees must support and advance the mission, value, tradition, the reputation, and image of the institution. He/she must understand that his/her responsibilities include guidance, oversight of the policies, donate generously, and influence others to contribute money for creating a large endowment for the institution. The trustee must master the arts of operational functions of an academic institution, and the challenges that might affect smooth functioning of the academic entity. He/she must be well informed about the institution and contribute in the design and execution of policies in the board meetings (AGB Report; n.d.).

Role of the president

The college president is the chief executive officer of the college. The board of trustee authorizes the president to execute all administrative and executive duties for the operation of the institution, and he/she is directly responsible for the overall policy direction of the college and share authority for its operation with the faculty. He/she makes policy recommendations to the board of trustee on all matters of the college such as standards for admissions of the students, the appointments and promotion of the faculty, the approval of academic programs, annual budget, strategies involving student enrollment management, academic quality, infrastructure, campus building programs, federal and state policy, and governance of the total institution. He/she is responsible for all reports that may be required by the board of trustees, local, state, and federal agencies. The president is also involved in local community development and plays a leadership role in the advancement of higher education in local, state, and national level. College president will actively involve in raising money for the institution and ensuring that all components of the institution are working together as a unified entity (Davis; 2000, Bowdoin ; n.d.).

Role of faculty

The major responsibilities of faculty in an academic institution is "to promote inquiry and advance the sum of human knowledge, to provide a general instruction to the students, and to develop experts for various branches of the public service" (Joughin 1969).

Faculty members teach students various subjects essential in their field of expertise and impart various skills for the survival of the pupils in the twenty-first century. They assist students how to gain the skills, develop intellectual mastery of the fields of studies whether it is sciences, humanities, arts, or music. The skill sets are the building block of mastering the arts and sciences that will ensure the learners to enhance the process of in-depth learning and meaningful application and transformation of the knowledge to problem solving through analytical interpretive acumen.

Faculty members must maintain their own developments in their expertise and continue active participation in research and other desirable scholarly activities so they can impart their student's current and cutting-edge development in their expertise. The main thrust of the faculty should be how to open the window of knowledge and provide guidance to follow the pathways to a successful understanding and interpretation of the information so that learners could decipher the secret that will enlighten the mind and enjoy the learning experience.

Faculty research is an integral part of teaching. Instruction must be supported by research, because a process of creating a knowledge base is research-dependent, and it helps the process and quality of instruction. Research faculty are a better teacher because they are always active in thinking process through analyses and interpretive domain, and more willing to use their knowledge during teaching in the classroom. Faculty research activities also provide opportunities to the students to develop their skills in research that allow them to be a better thinker and sharpen their critical thinking and analytical skills.

Faculty also plays an important role in the institutional services, which include serving on various institutional committees, student mentoring, academic coaching, and act as role models. They also serve on various local community affairs that forms bridges between community and institution of higher learning.

Role of faculty senate/association

Faculty senate/faculty association is an organizational entity comprising all faculty employed by an academic institution. This organization is the key voice of the faculty concerns, institutional direction and functions, and overall proponent of the central issues that govern and manage the smooth, seamless, and effective policies of operation of the institution. Faculty delegates its authority to the senate leaders who can communicate with the president and the board of trustees for the well-being of the institution and other related matters.

The faculty should lead the policies of curricular development, implementation, and academic programs and senate will oversee these curricular developments and get involved in the deliberation and final passage through the senate body and to the chief academic officer of the institution (provost) for final implementation of the curriculum. Senate will also suggest and advise the provost and the president for institutional budget and act as the champion of academic freedom and transparency.

Research project involving a national survey of AGB member institutions of higher learning conducted by the Association of Governing Boards of universities and colleges in 2009 to evaluate how boards, presidents, and faculty interact with one another by sharing ideas regarding policy matters that would allow a better governance of the academic institutions. In this project 2007 AGB member institutions received the survey instruments and 417 institutions responded to the survey. Surveys were sent to 2033 individuals at 2007 AGB member institutions; only 532 participants from 417 institutions completed the survey. Responses came from chief executive officers, chief academic officers, board chairs, and system heads. Besides survey instruments, telephone and in-person interviews were also conducted. Unfortunately, no faculty input was involved in this research (Schwartz et al. 2009).

Some findings of this research were

1. the board, president, and faculty lack mutual understanding and respect;
2. presidents did not favor interaction among board and faculty and are unwilling to allow or engage boards and faculty;

3. faculty and board members must be educated in governance and management policies; and
4. at least some members of the board must include experienced educators.

This research was poorly designed and somewhat inadequate, because the survey questions and interviews did not include the opinion of the faculty leaders, instead the design was based on the opinions of the administrative sectors such as presidents, chief academic officers, deans, board of trustees chairs, and system heads. Institutional governance is rested on three pillars: the board, the president, and the faculty. The third-pillar faculty is not included in this research design. Instead this project trusted the responses from administration about their perception regarding faculty, what they might say or believe the faculty should say about the survey questions.

Best practices for the shared governance in academic institutions

Stephen C. Bahls, president of Augustana College, Rock Island, Illinois, proposed five best practices that will make shared governance work in academic institutions (Bahls 2014).

According to Bahls (2014), board members, president, and faculty leaders must be engaged in planning a policy to delineate what shared governance is and how to implement them. Development of the policy must be based on open communication, trust, and respect. This collegial cooperative environment will create a positive goodwill among all parties involved for the smooth operation of the institution. The faculty should be responsible for the development of curriculum, integrity of the curricular activities, academic quality, and academic excellence. Faculty should be equally involved in the financial decisions taken by the board, and the board should encourage faculty contribution in this matter with openness. Fiduciary responsibility is one of the most important operational activities of the board and most of the times the board make financial and business decisions without consulting the faculty, as if the views of faculty are not at all important for the operation and well-being of the institution. These myopic visions create a very unhealthy environment to govern the institution. Once the trust and respect among each party are compromised, then the process of governance become a failed policy. The impact will affect the operation of the institution and it will endanger the idea and values of shared governance. The most important aspect of shared governance is developing systems of open communication where faculty members, board members, and administrators work together and implement strategic priorities.

Assess the state of shared governance and develop an action plan together to improve the quality and efficiency of the shared governance. The board and the president should encourage and support faculty governance of the academic programs and allow the faculty leaders to express their opinion freely and with no penalty. Open and full exchange of ideas between all parties will create an environment of trust and transparency that will allow formation of a cohesive, meaningful directives that will enhance effective operation of the institution. The board and the president should include faculty regarding institutional governance so that it will eliminate the distrust and apathy for the faculty (Bahls 2014).

Bahls (2014) advocated that the board members, president, and administration and faculty leaders should involve in serious discussion to set guidelines regarding what is shared governance and what isn't. They should support that the shared governance is one of the central issues in academic institutions. All participants must adhere to the principles of shared governance through open communication, trust, transparency, and mutual respect.

The faculty has the central role in academic policy and must manage the academic quality of the institution. Board members should be open to the ideas of faculty leaders about the financial decisions made by the board before enacting them. Faculty leaders, the president, board members should meet to discuss the state of the academic institution so that all parties will know potential shortcomings or challenges that might destabilize the institutional operation. The challenges that have the potential to destabilize the institutional operation must overcome through the strategies developed by the team effort of all concerned participants. Full and honest exchange of ideas among all parties regarding operational decision can help the institution overcome many obstacles and avoid pitfalls (Bahls 2014).

Analysis of various reports generated through national surveys regarding the interaction between board, president, and faculty provided a picture that revealed that they do not act as a cohesive group. Instead they show a divisive entity (Schwartz et al. 2009). National surveys provided two different pictures. One group of participants gave a picture where the board, president, and faculty showed a positive interaction between all parties, whereas the other group presented a negative picture of interaction between all parties.

The group that presented a negative picture showed that most board members, president, and faculty dislike to interact with each other. If some discussions would take place between them, a lot of tension and disagreement ensued. The board and president do not respect the faculty and faculty feel neglected by the attitude displayed by the board. Most boards do not want that faculty should be present in the board meeting and/or will not support that faculty to hold an active membership in the board. Also, all parties (the board, president, and faculty) agree that no one has enough time for interaction at meetings. The bottom line is that board and president do not believe faculty has an important role in governance of the academic institution. This sentiment of non-inclusiveness of faculty in the board meetings is the main theme present among HBCUs.

The other group stated that there is frequent interaction between the board, president, and faculty took place in an open, transparent engagement of ideas between all participants in a cordial and collegiate environment. Many board members and presidents supported the idea that faculty should be included in the board of trustee committees to govern the institutions (Schwartz et al. 2009).

From this analysis, each group looks at the central issue of interaction between the board, president, and faculty in a different light and perhaps not sure about the best practices to follow to extend faculty role in the governance of the institutional policies. This philosophical division in governance is a major barrier for effective operation of academic institutions, because the inclusiveness mentality is lacking in many of these board members and presidents. It is deplorable that some members of academic governing board do not give due respect and share of indebtedness of faculty in their views.

Institutional governance and HBCUs

The perspective on shared governance at Historically Black Colleges and Universities provide a stark picture of non-acceptance philosophy that differs greatly from other mainstream institutions. The private HBCUs are against inclusiveness of faculty sharing with institutional governance. Many institutions do not have the system in place to encourage and empower faculty senate/association, and do not believe there is a need to develop and implement institution-wide policy of faculty inclusiveness in the governance of the institution. Some of these institutions do not want to change the cultural practices that would open a free flow of ideas and information among faculty, board, and president that would enhance the practices of better governance. Phillips (2002) reported that the faculty at Jackson State University had no input in the academic decision-making process.

Gasman and Hilton (2010) used the AAUP censured data over twenty-five years to analyze the governance and academic freedom policies in HBCUs.

Eight institutions including Clark Atlanta University (2010), Stillman College (2009), Virginia's State University (2005), Benedict College (2005), Philander Smith (2004), Meharry Medical College (2004), University of District of Columbia (1998), and Talladega College (1986) were censured by the AAUP for violating the AAUP governing policies on academic freedom and governance issues. Majority institutions of higher education abide by the principles of academic freedom and shared governance policies formulated by AAUP organization. According to the AAUP (AAUP; n.d.) prescribed policies, "each academic institution should allow faculty to research with no constraint, should have freedom to teach materials of their expertise with no kind of indifference, after seven years exemplary service faculty should be given the tenure so he/she could work there permanently and they cannot be terminated without due cause or 'bona fide' financial exigencies."

Gasman and Hilton (2010) argue that HBCUs represent 3 percent of the nation's colleges and universities but eight HBCUs have been censured in the past twenty-five years show institutions are not following proper governance practices. Review of these censured HBCUs disclosed a systemic pattern where the denial of due process was rampant and presidents imposed a ban on freedom of speech and any negative criticism of the administration. In some cases, the faculty senate was dissolved. This dictatorial authority of the president of various institutions created an environment of fear, intimidation, coercion, and abuse of power throughout the academic sector, and took away the basic human right from the faculty. The board also played a major role by giving the president to make academic decisions without consulting or input from the faculty. All these eight academic institutions paid a high price to this heavy-handed authoritarian administration that led to the fiscal mismanagement, recruitment and retention problems, and warning from the accreditation agencies for poor governance.

The institution must practice sound governance policies essential for normal effective functioning of the institution. Effective governance of an institution is rested on three pillars: board of trustees, president, and faculty senate/association. Each of these pillars are interconnected and form a cohesive entity. If any of these three pillars lose its cohesiveness through discord or malfunction, then the unity of the system will collapse causing serious damage to the function of the institution. Many HBCUs are facing this problem. The board members and the president do not give importance to the opinion of the faculty as if the faculty has no business in the governance of the institution. The importance and role of faculty in the governance of HBCUs are minimal. On paper and verbal assertion that faculty opinion/suggestions are essential in governance of the institutions by the president in most HBCUs are given with a lot of fanfare and hoopla, but when the time comes to support or give credence to the faculty's concern, suggestion, and input, all the external posture of faculty inclusiveness in the governance of the institution is nothing but a hypocritical gesture of the part of the administration. Many HBCU presidents act like tribal chiefs/dictators and these leaders feel that whatever they're doing is the right medicine for the institutional operation and function. Any person who disagrees with the president's decision, he/she will be marked as disloyal to the institution policies and soon will receive a notice showing that the services of this individual is not needed and will be terminated. If the person has tenure, then his/her duties/responsibilities will be curtailed with a substantial reduction in salary.

HBCUs board members and presidents do not believe in the tenure system. Most private HBCUs institution presidents think giving tenure to the faculty is dangerous for the operation of the institution and interfere with their autocratic rule in the governance of the institution. Presidents think they are the masters and the faculty should act like their slaves. This unconscious remnant/vestiges of slave mentality persisted in American institutions.

Many HBCUs are in a financial crisis. This crisis is not only due to federal/state funding cuts, plus loan debacle or low enrollment. The mismanagement and huge compensation package of the president are responsible for this catastrophic effect on institutions.

For the well-being of the institution, the board of trustees and the president must follow the sound practices of good governance that include governing the institution in a guided pathway that leads to success and effective learning and productivity of learners and clients. In the past many boards of trustees at HBCUs instead of governing, the board took over the role of management that led to disastrous results. Stewardship should be the goal of the board (AGB Report, n.d.).

Selection of the board member is very important for the proper functioning of the university. Survey of the presidents showed that recruitment of board members familiar with the academia—its importance, requirement, fiscal policy, fiduciary responsibilities, and vision—by selecting a diverse and progressive, dynamic, and fiduciary responsible board, the institution can move forward to a successful and fiscally sound institution.

It is interesting to note that Spelman College and the Dillard University championed the wisdom of shared governance with faculty and academic freedom that led to a vibrant institution of enchanting environment where freedom of free speech, free-flowing ideas, and transparency of policies flourished and nurtured by the president and board members. The obvious result of these positive interactions between the board, president, faculty and all other stakeholders reap the benefit of academic excellence and receiving the highest-ranking institution among all HBCUs and in the national ranking of 81 among best liberal arts colleges. The success of Spelman College can be attributed to the wisdom in maintaining harmony along the three pillars of governance. All HBCUs should follow this wisdom so that the real transformation can happen to each of these deserving institutions of higher learning.

Black color complex

HBCUs were created during the Reconstruction era so that ex-slaves would have access to education. These schools were open for Blacks only, thus Black education system was following a segregated system where only Black students were admitted as Whites were not interested to enroll in those educational institutions. By default, segregation was practiced in these institutions. A new type of segregation started in many earlier HBCUs where skin tone became a force that separated people of same racial background. Thus segregated policy was used to deny dark-skinned Blacks to enroll in these HBCUs. For example, Spelman College, Fisk University, Atlanta University, Howard University, Hampton University, Wilberforce University, and other Black institutions followed these practices. Same light-skinned Blacks develop a strong racially segregated attitude against dark-skinned Blacks in the academic sector. Most prestigious schools like Spelman College "allegedly required passing a color test before being admitted" (Russell et al.; 1992, 28).

By the turn of the century, mulatto elite emerged as the intellectual and political leaders of Black community in America. W.E.B. Du Bois wrote in an essay where he called on Black community to produce a college-educated class whose mission would be to serve and guide the progress of the masses (Russell et al. 1992, 31). Du Bois designated twenty-one men and two women leaders who would lead the Black masses were mulatto except one, who had dark skin. These leaders represented DuBois's famous phrase "Talented Tenth." Du Bois strongly emphasized that these top 10 percent of Negro population will lead the Black masses to achieve full human rights. Booker T. Washington, W.E.B. Du Bois, Frederick Douglass, Benjamin Banneker, and many other successful leaders were all mulattos. "Du Bois's 'Talented Tenth' list made abundantly clear, possessing a degree of mixed ancestry was a definite asset when it came to being considered a voice for the Negro race" (Russell et al. 1992, 32).

American society has been controlled by Whites because they were in the helm of political power, educational hierarchy, attainment, and economical control. Black minorities endowed with light skin with European features received maximum privileges during the time of slavery and present times, allowed them to advance educationally and politically as well as occupationally over dark-skinned Blacks (Russell et al. 1992). These privileged opportunities resulted a pool of light-skinned Blacks who became the voice of freedom and equality for all minorities.

Black president of many HBCUs prefer light-skinned Black women or White women in their administrative circle. Some would prefer to recruit White women as the dean or provost even if they are not the best qualified person for the job. This kind of sexually oriented administrative selection process revealed both the conscious and unconscious desire of the president to feel that "he has made it."

Jill Nelson (1990) quoted in an article what filmmaker Spike Lee said, "whether black men admit it or not, they feel light-skinned women are more attractive than dark skinned, and they would rather see long hair than a short Afro, because that is closer to white women. That comes from being inundated with media from the time you were born that constantly fed you the white woman as the image of beauty. That is both conscious and unconscious" (Nelson 1990).

Politics in Academic operation

Hiring practices and influence of color in HBCUs

Hiring practices in HBCUs follow a guideline that encourages and supports color-defined policies. If Black candidates are available, then the job should go to Black candidate for a faculty position regardless of their academic credentials. As the demand of qualified Black PhD candidates are high but the supply of well-qualified Black PhD personnel are low, then job goes down for non-Black candidates. A discrete social model has been evolved through the years during 1950 through 1990 by the educators that define the color line in HBCUs. Afro-American Blacks are the "brothers/sisters." Foreign-born African-American Blacks are the "undefined brother." Asians are known as a "Brown brother/sisters" and Whites are called White.

During the hiring faculty personnel, the administrators will look for "brothers" if no brothers are available, then the panel will look for undefined brother. If that is not in the pool, then a White or a Brown brother will be considered for the position. The pool of candidates need to be defined here so that a better picture can be seen to understand how the personnel are selected through the selection process.

PhD from White universities: White graduates from tier three and four White universities will not get academic positions in White universities they target positions in community colleges, four-year White and Black colleges. Many of these graduates get positions at HBCUs institutions and they accept the job reluctantly. White faculty members at HBCUs institutions feel like a social outcast in their own community because they are working in HBCUs. They are working just to pick up a check necessary for their survival. Few feel they belong to these institutions. Many of these professionals apply to other institutions including community colleges so they could get out of HBCUs. But majority professors are stuck with the situation and they cannot get a position in the community colleges or PWIs. Many experienced that their association with HBCUs play a negative influence detrimental for hiring by the White institutions. The administrators of HBCUs institutions also treat White faculty bad and rarely, a White professional will be selected for administrative positions. Those selected for administrative positions they act like puppets because they do not have the right to exercise their authority. These White professionals who are selected must play the game of "yes, boss." If any of these professionals criticize the authoritarian boss, then the person would be moved out of the office with no cause. Most HBCUs administrations are run by presidents who do not follow a democratic way in running their business. This problem is one of the most destructive force that is crippling HBCUs.

PhD from White universities: Afro-American students graduated from tier three or four institutions rarely get positions in White colleges and universities. But they are hired in HBCUs and become the deans/top administrators/faculty leaders. They are the mainstream intelligentsia who run most of the HBCUs.

Asians who received a doctorate degree from tier three and four White universities do not get positions in White universities because of their race/national origin/gender bias/language/accent etc., but many are hired in the small White colleges and HBCUs. However, Asian graduates from tier one White institutions are hired in tier one and two White schools as a research faculty. Seldom have they received tenure as regular teaching faculty. Research faculty positions are usually funded through government/private foundations as such tenured positions are not granted to them.

PhD from HBCUs institutions: many Afro-American Blacks, African Blacks, and Asians received their doctoral degree from PhD granting HBCUs universities. Most of these universities do not have national ranking, and they are considered tier five institutions. For example, Howard University is the highest-ranking among HBCUs institutions in the country but have earned a ranking of 172 out of 200 ranked research universities (The Center for Measuring University Performance (MUP); n.d.).

These graduates are hired in four-year HBCUs. African-American graduates receive administrative jobs in the HBCUs; however, the Asian graduates will receive no administrative positions because of their origin. White universities and four-year colleges rarely hire Asian doctoral graduates from HBCUs because White institutions have strong racial bias against immigrants and they believe that HBCU products are inferior to their own graduates. Majority of these Asian professionals are hired at HBCUs and represent the Science, Technology, Engineering, and Mathematics (STEM) fields. They work very hard to get research grants so that institution can build a better and modern laboratory infrastructure that would enhance research and teaching capabilities and train students so they could compete with the White elites. From 1960 to 2000 these Asian academicians trained and prepared the largest number of African-American medical professionals and scientists. Their contribution, dedication, and hard work has never been recognized by the HBCUs because of racism.

Promotion and tenure process in private HBCUs

A tenure and promotion committee comprises with tenured faculty are at least ranked associate professor or higher. Each school/division will nominate one person to the committee. The ideal person to be selected from each school/division must be a professional who has attained highest academic distinction based on scholarly activities, leadership abilities, community service, and collegiality. But in most private HBCUs, this rule of academic excellence is not practiced. Instead, the dean selects his/her choice of a faculty member to represent the school/division, is based on nepotism, favoritism, inept, discriminatory, and outright subjugated faculty. The dean selects a member who will carry the wishes of the dean to the promotion and tenure committee proceedings. The deans are the academic dictator in the respective schools/division. If the prospective faculty who is an accomplished academician based on his/her scholarly productivity and instructional excellence, he/she may not be promoted if the dean does not like the candidate because of his/her outspoken personality and/or academic superiority. Because the deans are selected by the president of the institution based on academic subjugation and acquiescence policy, and the loyalty oath of absolute obedience, then most deans are not intellectually qualified to be the leaders of the college. This policy of instilling inferior academic leadership personnel in private HBCUs are destroying the academic rigor essential for the institutions to be competitive in academic sectors. The graduates coming out from these schools are not prepared well to compete in the global job market place or professional arena.

Each school/division dean submits his/her candidate to represent the school to the office of the vice president of academic affairs/provost, and this office forms a committee that will select faculty applicants applied for promotion and tenure process. Faculty submit their dossier documenting academic qualification, student evaluation, peer evaluation and outside professional support letters, scholarly activities including article reprints, community activities, and other materials of importance. Dossier also contain the deans and chairperson's evaluation of the candidate. The selected promotion and tenure committee members by the vice president of academic affairs/provost to evaluate each candidate's portfolio and report their findings to the academic affairs office. Sometimes, the tenure and promotion committee members meet and pass their findings to the committee chairperson elected by the vice president of academic affairs/provost. This confidential report is evaluated by the vice president of academic affairs/provost and transmit its findings with the VP-academic affairs/provost comments and recommendation goes to the president's office for his/her approval or denial of the faculty candidate's application for promotion and tenure.

This is the normal operational process as delineated in the faculty handbook. However, this normal operational process is not followed because of various conflicts that has been practiced regularly in the promotion/tenure proceedings:

1. If the dean is not very favorable about the applicant for promotion/tenure due to applicant's higher intellectual productivity and outspoken personality that undermine the dictatorial, authoritative style of the dean or White/Brown brother syndrome, which points to anti-intellectual/racial conflict of the dean that clouds his/her judgment, then the prospective candidate's application for promotion/tenure will be denied.

2. The dean's power is supreme because the president selected him/her for a deanship position because of his/her allegiance and academic slave mentality, which allows the president to carry out his/her vision about the institution. The academic excellence and high-powered intellectual development is the essence of an institution of higher learning; however, no one believes in it, because that is contrary to the practices followed in the institution.

3. The collusion of the dean, provost/VPAA and the president creates an environment of mediocrity and Afro-centric bias pulling down the academic productivity, excellence, and competitiveness in HBCUs.

Customer service and education

Customer service is a marketing technique used in a business where the main thrust of the seller is to please the customer so that the organization will benefit financially and develop a positive experience for the buyer that would motivate the buyer to come back again to the seller for more merchandise to purchase. This helps the business to create and maintain a loyal customer base, which will translate into higher profit and rapid inventory clearance for the business. This successful model is used by many organizations including large national chain stores. They follow a motto "customer is always right." If the customer is not happy about an item, then the merchant would be happy to take back the product and return the money to the customer, if he/she chooses that option. This business practice is to "hook" the customers for more business transactions and develop a preferential attitude about the seller.

Many public and private HBCUs institutions of higher learning are using this marketing technique to hold and keep their student recruits. This model works well in business ventures but to apply in an educational enterprise creates an environment that distracts and sabotage the process of academic integrity and excellence. The financially struggling institutions are desperate to keep the student body, at any cost. The administrators feel that "good customer service" toward the student body will help the institution retain these students. Retention is the key for the survival of the institution. The government grants and loans depend on student retention. If an institution experiences low retention rate, then the federal government grants and loans will be affected and fiscal squeeze levied on the institution. To avoid this scenario, the institution created an environment where students feel an upper hand over the academic environment of the institution. The "customer is always right" philosophy forces the administration to impose various rules on faculty to accommodate the wishes of the students, which results into academic dishonesty and grade inflation. Once students know the administration will always support their whims/demands in the guise of "customer service," the students take advantage of the situation various ways.

The academic culture is tainted with non-academic, entertainment filled activities in most colleges and universities. Present college and university students think they deserve everything and do not have to do any hard work or effort to get this privilege. They are called entitlement generation. They expect good grades because they have paid for it. Hard work and ethical standards are not in their vocabulary. They go to college or universities because their parents want them to have a college education so they could learn something valuable, which will ensure a steady income and a good living.

Majority of students are glued to their cell phone and/or iPad. These modern electronic gadgets are excellent tools for educational instructions but instead, students use them for entertainment such as listening music, chat, text for hours but nothing educational.

Cell phone usage

Cell phone has revolutionized the way we communicate with each other. The mobility, versatility, and affordability of cell phones made our communication system one of the best scientific wonders in our digital existence. We cannot live without it. Younger adults between twenty-eight to twenty-nine age group and college-bound students use the cell phones in a variety of ways. The Pew Research

Center published a paper about the cell phone activities in America (Duggen 2013).

The demographic analysis found that African-Americans and Hispanics use the cell phone and its various capabilities much more than Whites. The table describes the various usage for cell phone (Table 1).

Table 1. Performing various activities on cell phone by race/ethnicity (percentages of cell phone owners).[20]

Race/ethnicity	Video chatting	Text messaging	Accessing Internet	Mobile email	Downloading apps	Listening music	Directions/Location-Related services
White-Non-Hispanic	19	79	56	52	48	42	49
Black-Non-Hispanic	20	85	72	59	60	61	51
Hispanic	32	87	67	53	52	64	55

Colleges and university students used a cell phone for their entertainment, Internet access, instructional purposes, and other necessary activities. Cell phone use inside the classrooms is usually regulated so that students will not be distracted during the class. Many HBCUs do not have a strict policy toward the cell phone usage in the classrooms. Many students abuse the cell phone usage in the class. They use them for entertainment purpose, even when the class is in session. Each institution must develop a strict policy for classroom usage because the students will abuse the privileges of using a cell phone in the classroom. Evidence suggests that cell phone usage during a class session disturb the whole instructional process. Cell phones must be banned in the classroom usage.

---

[20] Cell phone activities 2013. (http://pewinternet.org/Reports/2013/Cell-Activities.aspx)

The entitlement generation

Games students play

This twenty-first century students belong to entitlement generation. They believe they own everything and it is their right to have them regardless of the cost. The parents are responsible for their birth, and it is their duty to provide everything to their offspring. All secondary students demand from their parents that they are entitled to have an iPhone, iPad, and other social media friendly gadgets is there in the market. The parents must provide them because it is necessary for them to have it so they could be a part of their generational milieu. Most parents oblige their growing-up children so they would feel they have done their parental duty. This generation of students extended their entitlement rights to education. In the school, they think grades are to be given to them by the teachers because they are forced to attend the secondary schools due to state laws. These students expect that teachers must give them good grades regardless of their effort and they are entitled to get passing grades at least in each classes they are enrolled. This pathetic attitude and culture by our new generation is reflected well in US fifteen-year-old students' performance in the PISA/TIMMS international tests. US ranking in 2012 PISA test average reading score of 498 (20th place), average math score 481 (30th place) and average science score 501 (23rd place).

This entitlement generation when moved to the college of their choice carry with them this mentality of "give me" to a next level of demand. In the college these students proclaim that "they deserve to get good grades, because they are paying for it." Even students have the audacity to tell the faculty members that "I am paying your salary, and you must serve me." This is a new twist of the saga of "Customer Care" philosophy some college presidents who believe educational institutions are a business enterprise.

President's Playbook: How to bump up retention

State of the college union address by the president of the institution tells the faculty that student retention is one of the most important pillars that supports and stabilizes the economic survival of the institution. More retention of students means more revenue for the institution, which provides the salary of the faculty and staff. Higher retention of the students allows the institution to receive funding from the state and federal government, and keep federal government's accountability requirements at bay.

The president's speech continue to hammer his/her faculty audience that if student retention falters, then the monetary supply line will squeeze to a trickle that will jeopardize jobs you are enjoying and we must do everything so that students will continue to stay here with us. The president again reminds the audience that customer service is very important in this institution and implores that all faculty must live and breathe with the philosophy of these services for the well-being of our students. The president conclude his/her state of the Union speech, "We are here because of the students, if they decide not to attend our institution, then we have no place to go. We must do everything so they could stay with us. This is our goal and we are here to serve."

The president of the college sends a subliminal message to the faculty audience that serves all needs of the student clientele's; if that is not provided to them, then you have no business in this place.

The game deans play

During the dean's meeting he/she reminds the faculty that student retention is very important for the survival of the institution. The faculty is responsible for the classroom instruction and imparting knowledge to the students so they are learning something in the classroom that will help them be successful citizens. Students must learn in the classroom that justify their progress toward earning a degree in their chosen field of studies. The dean asked each faculty to do their job better so that the students will be prepared to face the global competition and win the race. At the same time the dean emphasizes that student evaluation of the teacher is the most important factor for keeping the faculty in the institution. If your students give you poor ratings, then you will be dismissed from your position. The faculty peer evaluation is not very important in the process because the institutional policy dictates Customer Care, which assures student retention is the benchmark criterion for keeping your job. "Give me" generation in college expects that their teachers will help them pass the courses they are enrolled. They're too busy in networking through Facebook, texting with their fellow peers, and spend in an enormous amount of time in social media that became an addictive lifestyle of youths in America today. This compulsive, behavioral nature has robbed the young intellectuals the desire and drive to flourish in academia.

The millennial generation dislike rigorous academic environment and developed a repulsion to the faculty who believe in academic rigor, hard work, and "tough love" attitude. The demanding faculty faces the wrath of student hostility toward them and most of the times receive poor student evaluation because of their academic demands. These are the groups of faculty who will be in the chopping block for the elimination from the institution. In an academic environment, the rigorous, demanding, and hardworking faculty should be the leaders for progress and achievement and should be rewarded. Instead, in this customer-centric academic environment, the faculty are treated as the outcast and will be dismissed from their jobs.

The game faculty plays

The faculty learns the "survival of the fittest" principles in academia. They realize that customer-centric educational policy in the institution is a veiled coercive and intimidation technique used by the administration to dictate the faculty to "loosen up" academic integrity and rigor and pursue a path to serve the needs and demands of students. Through this action, faculty trap themselves into a corruptive shackle of practices, which permit them less rigorous academic standards, grade inflation, and other anti-intellectual activities that do not support learning. These practices allow higher percentages of students passing the courses even though they did not learn much and master the materials of importance for the course. Faculty "served their master" and received the "blessings" from the master that proclaims "good teacher" and positive student ratings. Some faculty members who believed compromising academic integrity is not acceptable and only passed the students who earned their grades through hard work, received negative student ratings, which would affect their jobs.

During an economic downturn in the country if supply is greater than the demands, then the supply side will always lose. The number of faculty available for job market is always higher than the available faculty positions, which creates an intense competition to get a job in academic sector. This intense competition forces faculty to hold onto their jobs at any cost even if that leads to follow some unethical practices.

The administrators in private colleges and universities use this economic leverage to buy faculty. The faculty become stooges of the administrators. If the president of the college or university is a strong believer of authoritarian governance of the institution, then the faculty must follow the dictates, otherwise will be terminated without cause. The scenario depicted before described how an institution of higher learning can boost the retention rate. Larger number of students will pass the courses due to faculty acquiescence to grade inflation, lower academic standards, and other anti-intellectual activities. Higher passing rate will allow students to continue their academic pursuit and help boost the retention of students in the institution.

The corruption that has entrenched in academic institutions downgrades our colleges and universities across America. Our graduates are not competitive in a global arena. To maintain American superiority in science, medicine, engineering, agriculture, and other fields, we must address the serious issues of corruption in an academic enterprise and do our best to eliminate these practices so we can march forward in the twenty-first century as the leader and a beacon of hope in this world.

How to bump up the graduation rate

Graduation rate in an academic institution is one of the most important benchmark for the existence of the college/university. It is associated with the success of the institution, its program, and its ability to produce graduates who would be successful to procure jobs in their respective fields of studies/profession. Governmental agencies provide financial help to the academic institutions and expect that the institution will prepare students well so they could be successful and be a productive citizen of this country. The accreditation agencies certify the institutions as the well qualified entity to provide and train students for various skills necessary to get, keep, and successful execution of the skills for a particular job in any fields essential in a society.

The governmental agencies and accreditation agency look at the graduation rate of an academic institution they are supporting. If the graduation rate drops below the national average, then the red flag goes up against an institution unable to maintain required standards. The institution receives citation showing that they are faltering in their institutional responsibility/efficiency and put on "probation" or "warning," so that institution can "fix" the problems within a specific time. If the institution cannot fix the problems, then they will lose the financial help from the government and withdrawal of certification from the accreditation agency. The institution is in jeopardy and students will abandon this institution, which might lead to closure of the institution.

Federal government allows students a six-year time frame to earn a four-year college degree and provide financial aids to the students so they could graduate from college and earn a degree. This six-year time frame is commonly used to calculate graduation rate for all colleges and universities in US. In the year 2010, 48 percent students on average graduated from all colleges and universities in US and graduation rate rose to 59 percent in the year 2015. Spelman College, the highest ranking HBCUs liberal arts college in the nation, had a graduation rate of 70 percent in 2010 and in 2015 rose to 76 percent. However, majority HBCU's six-year graduation rate ranged from

5% to 42.3%. Graduation rate in many HBCUs need to improve so they could be considered institutions important for the education of youths and must be preserved as a large number of Black students attend these institutions (The Atlanta Journal-Constitution 2018).

To reverse this trend, some presidents of HBCUs followed a practice of bumping up graduation rate by creating a new curricular design where candidates failed to pass the program certification requirements by the accreditation/licensure organization, and are given a four-year degree in the liberal arts program. This practice of giving a degree in liberal arts program has been in use for a long time in the history of American education. HBCU's presidents borrowed this curricular design from big White universities that have been practicing this unethical and anti-intellectual arrangement for a long time.

Athletic programs bring millions of dollars to the big universities every year. Each top-ranked athlete in the university is considered as a giant cash cow, which will generate millions to the coffer of the university. These superstar students are nurtured by the university more than the Nobel laureates or great minds of academic geniuses walking in the corridors of ivory towers of knowledge. These athletes of extraordinary talents get a degree from the renowned university without attending the classes they are enrolled. Many superstar graduates confessed that they have difficulty in reading and writing but they have been awarded a bachelor's degree in liberal arts studies. This is an infamy in academia!

It is a common practice for students dropping out from the programs where rigorous intellectual efforts are necessary, and join non-challenging, diluted curricular requirements such as liberal arts studies program, so they could earn a four-year bachelor's degree from a college or a university and become a part of the educated society.

Many top administrators at HBCUs encourage the dropouts from hard-core academic programs to become a part of educated society by joining the liberal studies program and graduate on time. This way the percentage of dropouts will decrease and graduation rate will increase. Politics of student retention and student graduation rate among HBCUs are ruining the academic rigor, integrity, and value system. The net result of these anti-intellectual endeavors supported by corrupted few in institutional leadership is destroying the status and good name of HBCUs.

Examples of mismanagement, corruption, and fraud in HBCUs

Alabama State University: Recently the institution has gone through a forensic audit ordered by the State of Alabama legislature. The report of the audit discovered over $2.5 million worth of contracts issued by the institution with no tangible deliverable stipulated in the contract. A board member along with his family ran a sports foundation and milked $864,000 from the university between 2007 and 2013 (Stodghill 2015).

Alcorn State University: The charismatic President Dr. Christopher Brown of Alcorn State University was forced to resign from the presidency by the Mississippi College Board and Ethics Commission because of purchasing violations involving more than 795,000 dollars. Besides purchasing violations, the investigation also revealed that renovation of the president's house was undertaken without bids, which is illegal according to the state procurement laws (Stodghill 2015).

South Carolina State University: The Federal Bureau of Investigation (FBI) launched a federal corruption charges against the board of trustees Chairman Jonathan Pinson and university police chief Michael Bartley for receiving kickbacks from a land sale deal worth of three million dollars.

Paine College: George C. Bradley, president of Paine College, used his authority with the board of trustee to secure lines of credits by using college's endowment fund. This improper activity triggered a financial meltdown crisis in the eyes of the Southern Association of Colleges and Schools Commission on Colleges (SACSCOC) for accreditation and imposed a probation status for ten standard violations by the institution (Stodghill 2015).

Howard University: When the university was suffering from faculty furloughs, low enrollment, the deterioration of physical infrastructure like classrooms, dormitory, and laboratory buildings,

President Dr. Ribeau of the university acted as Santa Claus to reward bonuses of over 1.1 million dollars to his lackeys. This fiscal irresponsibility and mismanagement reaffirmed Dr. Bill Cosby's assessment of these academic leaders as "duplicitous, extolling platitudes of educating the next generation while perpetrating actions that were nothing less than destructive to the students who trusted them with their future and money" (Stodghill 2015, 194).

Twenty HBCUs presidencies were either vacant or in inhabited by some recycled recruits. Several presidents lost their jobs before even finishing their first contract while others left the job. Dr. David Wilson (Morgan State University) and Joseph Silver (Alabama State University) were both terminated by the board of a trustee for fiscal mismanagement.

Shaw University of North Carolina's Dr. Irma McClaurin quit her job after eleven months on the job. Tuskegee University President Dr. Gilbert L. Rochon resigned the presidency after three years at Tuskegee, and Dr. Matthew Jenkins became interim president. Stillman College President Ernest MacNealey served since 1997, was ended by the board due to sagging enrollment, low employee morale, and high turnover and strained ties with business community. Norfolk State University's Dr. Tony Atwater was fired by the board after two years on the job following poor marks by the university accreditation agency (Stodghill 2015).

Recent disclosures from the accreditation agency

Southern Association of Colleges and Schools Commission on Colleges (SACSCOC) board of trustee placed St. Augustine University, Raleigh, North Carolina, on warning because the institution had failed to demonstrate compliance with core requirement 2.11.1 (Financial resources and stability, December 17, 2015. SACSCOC; 2016).

Bennett College for Women Greensboro, North Carolina, received a "Warning" because the institution had failed to demonstrate compliance with comprehensive standard 3.10.1 (Financial stability of the principles of accreditation, December 17, 2015).

In June 16, 2016, SACSCOC announced that Alabama State University, Montgomery, Alabama, has been removed from Warning status. Bluefield College, Bluefield, Virginia, has been removed from Probation. South Carolina State University Orangeburg, South Carolina, and the University of North Carolina at Chapel Hill, North Carolina, have been removed from Probation.

In June 23, 2016, Tuskegee University, Tuskegee, Alabama, was placed on Warning because the university failed to show comprehensive standard 3.3.1.1 (Institutional effectiveness: educational program, comprehensive standard 3.10.1; financial stability, comprehensive standard 3.10.2 [financial aid audits]; and federal requirement 4.7 [Title IV program responsibilities]). Warning was removed on June 2017.

Elizabeth City State University, Elizabeth City, North Carolina, was placed on Warning because of unsolicited information generated through media resources alleging "non-compliance with standards regarding administrative/academic officers, personnel appointments and evaluations, admissions, student records and control of finances" (SACSCOC 2016). The college is still on Warning as of June 23, 2017.

The SACSCOC board of trustees voted to Paine College, Augusta, Georgia, from membership for failure to comply with core requirements 2.11.1 (financial resources and stability) on June 23, 2016.

Bennett College, Greensboro, North Carolina, maintained accreditation status for "good cause" and placed on Probation for twelve months. This will be the last year to clear the financial problem by raising four million dollars and boost student attendance to at least 450 students. President Phyllis Worthy Dawkins believed Bennett College will raise the money and increase student enrollment so that college can claim full accreditation status.

Ford Valley State University, Ford Valley, Georgia, is in Warning status.

Southern University and A&M College at Baton Rouge, Louisiana, received Warning for noncompliance in core requirement 2.8 (faculty), 3.3.1.1 (institutional effectiveness), Federal requirement 4.1 and 4.5 (student achievement and student complaints respectively) (SACSCOC, June 23, 2017).

St. Augustine University continued to maintain accreditation status for "good cause" and placed on Probation for one year (SOCSCOC, December 2017).

Paine College has been reinstated for accreditation by the US District Court for the Northern District of Georgia, but still it will be on probation by SACSCOC.

Cheyney University, Cheyney, Pennsylvania, is the nation's oldest HBCU, and it is on Probation since 2015. The Middle States Commissions on Higher Education extended its probation for another year so that the state university could fix its financial and administrative problems. Besides accreditation problems, Cheyney is also under investigation by the Justice Department for mishandling twenty-nine million dollars in financial aids funds. The university is planning to select interim President Aaron A. Walton as the permanent president (Phillips and Snyder 2017).

Unfolding mismanagement of funds at Bethune-Cookman University

Joe Petrock, board of trustee chairman, at Bethune-Cookman University said BCU has formed a presidential search committee that includes staff, alumni, board members, and students (Robbins and Jarmusz 2017). The faculty will not be a part of the presidential search committee. This direct omission of the faculty shows the chairman of the board of a trustee do not believe faculty is an important part of the governance process at Bethune-Cookman University. Edison O. Jackson, former president, did not value the importance of faculty in the governance process and his chairman of the board of trustee also did not believe the faculty has an important role in it. This type of thinking led to erosion of the institutional integrity and effectiveness.

Recent exposure of financial irresponsibility and mismanagement by the president Jackson along with the support from the board chairman Joe Petrock might have positioned the Bethune-Cookman

University under the radar of the Southern Association of Colleges and Schools Commission on Colleges (SACSCOC) and the accreditation agency will pay attention on the Comprehensive Standard 3.10.1 (Financial stability) of the university in the upcoming institutional reaffirmation cycle.

President Jackson and the board of trustees ignored the plea from B-CU alumnus Robert Delancy to be transparent about the dormitory construction project, but Jackson refused Delancy's request and moved him out from the board of trustee committee. A few alumni and board of trustees were wondering about schools finances, regarding dormitory project, but President Jackson ignored their concerns and removed them from the board membership.

Seth Robbins and T.S. Jarmusz, two journalists from *Daytona Beach News-Journal* opened the secrets of the dormitory deal at B-CU. Their investigative report revealed that new dorms will cost the school $306 million (Robbins and Jarmusz 2017). Reporters found out that the dormitory will cost the school more than $300 million when paid off in forty years. Fitch Ratings agency downgraded schools credit-rating three times by June 2017 because of B-CU's "aggressive level of debt." The financing agreement deal was structured in such a way that monthly payment for the lease will jump $470,000 a month to a high of about $840,000, which will be $10 million a year.

President Jackson and his top thirteen (13) administrators received a combined compensation of $2.69 million, which is an average of $207,000 for each employee this year. The previous year President Jackson and his eight (8) executives received a compensation of $1.4 million, which is an average of $175,000. Fifty (50) employees were paid at least one hundred thousand dollars or more this year. Majority of the faculty earned less than fifty thousand dollars per year, when a few chosen ones of President Jackson collected more than a hundred thousand dollar a year salary (Robbins and Jarmusz 2017). Distinguished professors brought millions of dollars of grant money from federal government sources such as NIH, NSF, DOE, and others for research, instruction, and improvement of laboratory infrastructure and dedicated service to the institution for over thirty years could not even get seventy thousand dollars a year salary under President Jackson. Distinguished professor is a "Brown Brothers," was it due to racism? No wonder why Edison O. Jackson refused to have forensic auditing done at B-CU.

Johnny McCray Jr., a trustee from 2007 to 2016, said, "Jackson had a way of buying people, and when I say 'buying' . . . I mean Dr. Jackson gave people honorary doctorate degrees almost routinely" (Robbins and Jarmusz, February 3, 2018. *The Daytona Beach News-Journal*). President Jackson gave a bonus of $110,000 to Hakim Lucas, vice president for institutional advancement. A 1.5 million loan issued to an undisclosed recipient, and this loan was mistakenly credited as a gift according to the B-CU's board of trustee meeting minutes (Robbins and Jarmusz 2018).

The Bethune-Cookman University sued ex-president Jackson and Hakim Lucas for corruption and fraud. Heron Development Group sued Bethune-Cookman University over a scuttled off-campus student housing deal worth millions of dollars. All these activities conducted by President Jackson alleged by the board of trustees and the board are acting like an entity oblivious of these activities. This is enough reason to believe the board is impotent to act and failed about the duties of trusteeship and should be removed from the board. A new set of individuals with backgrounds in education, business, corporate leadership, entrepreneurs, law, and fund-raising should be selected to create a dynamic board that will run the university.

The Accreditation Commission for Education in Nursing notified Bethune-Cookman University in 2015 that nursing program may lose its accreditation if the university cannot achieve higher passing rate in the state licensing examination. The passing rate for B-CU nursing students was around 50%, when the national average was around 92%. State of Florida requires first-time test takers must pass the test within 10 percentage point of the national average passing rate. If an institution failed to achieve the passing rate for two years in a row, they would be placed in probation and, in some cases, may lose their accreditation. B-CU administration promised to improve the passing rate by incorporating much more rigorous academic standards so that students can pass the licensing exam.

On February 8, 2018, Florida Board of Nursing placed Bethune-Cookman University nursing program on probation when half of its twenty-eight students failed to the national licensing examination in 2017. The national average passing rate for 2017 was 90%. Since 2010 Bethune-Cookman University's nursing program passing rate that reached within 10 percentage point of the national average passing rate only in 2012, when B-CU students passing rate was 87%. Rest of the years B-CU scored below average the national passing rate (Jarmusz 2018).

President Jackson supported the customer service philosophy in keeping students and graduation rate. This model supports an erosion of educational rigor and excellence, which destroy faculty authority and academic integrity. To increase the retention and graduation rate, the institution is forced to dilute their academic curriculum, lower rigorous implementation of learning atmosphere and accountability, which will lower the students' ability to master the subject, critical thinking ability, and foster poor productivity and incompetence. This anti-intellectual environment encourages mediocrity. Probation of B-CU's nursing program is a direct evidence that erosion of academic rigor has destroyed the academic programs and ruined the life of students who wanted to be a registered nurse. As predicted, the Southern Association of Colleges and School Commission on Colleges placed B-CU on Probation on June 14, 2018 for non-compliance with Core Requirements.

Institutional corruption is destroying the core of academic enterprise at B-CU through the incompetence of the chairman, dean, provost, and the president. These educational hara-kiri at B-CU must stop so that the legacy of Dr. Mary MacLeod Bethune could be protected and preserved.

Why HBCUs are in trouble

Fourteen Historically Black Colleges and Universities (HBCUs) between the years 2000 and 2013 had only one administrative head running the operation of those institutions during the entire thirteen years. In contrast, seventeen institutions changed leadership over five times during these thirteen years (Toldson and Cooper 2014). Too much turnover in administrative head led to trouble for the academic institution and believed poor institutional governance and financial mismanagement are the root cause.

HBCUs also have trouble with the accreditation agency. For example, in 2014, Southern Association of Colleges and Schools Commission on Colleges (SACSCOC) placed Alabama State University and Allen University on warning status, and placed Paine College and South Carolina State University on probation. Wilberforce University received a "show cause order" from the North Central Association of Colleges and Schools (Toldson and Cooper 2014).

In all academic institutions, faculty promotion and tenure is an important measure of using proper human capital for maximum productivity and scholarship. Faculty members who have achieved academic rank of associate and full professor are considered as the most productive and scholarly individuals in the institution and carry high esteem among his colleagues and administration. Among HBCUs, on average 43 percent faculty members are full professors or associate professors. Many HBCUs do not use these valuable human capitals for instructional practices. For example, a high percentage of students are being taught by low-ranking faculty members or non-tenure track instructors at HBCUs (Toldson and Cooper 2014).

In many HBCUs the deans/provost select assistant professors to the chairmanship positions in major science areas bypassing associate and full professors because of favoritism. This action is not only anti-intellectual attitude but also reflect top administrator's quality of judgment and intellect. HBCUs also show extensive racial bias against its faculty who are not African-Americans. Gasman (2013) analyzed NCSE-2011 data of faculty by race/ethnicity and their tenure/tenure-track status among HBCUs found that non-Black faculty are seldom awarded tenure. Most tenured and tenure-track faculty belong to Blacks only (Table 2). Only 15.4% Asian faculty and 2% Hispanic faculty received tenure.

Table 2. Tenure status among faculty by race
and ethnicity in HBCUs: 2011[21]

Racial Groups/ Ethnicity	National with Tenure	National with Tenure Track	HBCU with Tenure	HBCU with Tenure Track
Asian/American Indian/ Alaskan/Pacific Islander	9.4%	13.5%	15.4%	8.3%
Black	4.0%	7.0%	57.0%	64.0%
Hispanic	4.0%	5.0%	2.0%	3.0%
White	84.0%	74.0%	27.0%	25.0%

In addition, almost never an Asian or Hispanic full professor will be appointed in any administrative position like associate dean or dean even if they are the most qualified and productive faculty in research, teaching, and getting grants. These exclusionary practices are very common among HBCUs. Academic excellence and merit are supposed to be color neutral but at HBCUs it is not.

In 2015, there were 102 HBCUs of which fifty-one were public institutions and the remaining fifty-one were private nonprofit institutions. In 2015, non-Black students attending HBCUs made up 22 percent. Black students attending HBCUs fell from 18% in 1978 to 9% in 2015. Over time, the percentage of bachelor's and master's degrees awarded by HBCUs to Black students fell. In the 1976–77 HBCUs awarded 35% of the bachelor's degree and 21% master's degrees to Black students, but in 2014–15, only 14% bachelor's degrees and 6% master's degrees were awarded to Black candidates (NCES Fast Facts; n.d.). These downward trends among Black students attending HBCUs and receiving fewer bachelors and master's degrees tell some ominous conditions lay ahead.

---

[21] Adapted from Gasman (2013). Total tenured or tenured track faculty at HBCUs is 5,694 (NCES 2011) as cited in Gasman (2013), Retrieved from: http://www. gse.upenn.edu/pdf/cmsi/Changing_Face_HBCUs.pdf

The higher education act of 1965 established an instrument to analyze and evaluate the ability of an institution's students to manage their debt, commonly called the cohort default rate (CDR). If an institution's federal student loan CDR exceeds 30 percent for three consecutive years, then that institution will lose its eligibility to take part in the federal direct loan and Federal Pell Grant programs. Student loan default rate is very important for an institution because if its students do not pay back the money they have borrowed, then the institution will be barred from taking part in the Pell grants and loan program, which are sustaining the HBCUs because over 70% of students receive federal financial aid to cover tuition, fees, and other expenses to attend college. Institutional survival depends on these grants and loan programs (Toldson and Cooper 2014).

Miller (2017) reported that 49 percent African-American students defaulted on a federal student loan borrowed during their undergraduate studies; many of them matriculated in HBCU institutions.

Default rate can be a good indicator for academic performance. Higher default rates suggest graduates/college attendees could not pay the loan or avoid paying back their educational loan. This may be due to various factors such as unemployment, poverty, family problems, or subpar employment. A large number of HBCU graduates work outside their field of training/expertise suggest they may not be competitive in expertise even though there is a strong emphasis to use minority graduates who are well trained.

Why top Black students do not go to HBCUs

Black colleges lost top Black students to White colleges and universities in the North, and some in the South after the *Brown versus Board of Education* decision in 1954. The top 10 percent Black students could go to White schools of their choice because White institutions opened their arms to accept Black students in their institutions to show they do not believe in segregation policies of the past era, and also to comply with the federal government's thrust toward desegregation, and monetary benefit linked with the new educational policy of racial integration and inclusiveness to maintain diversity. This policy of desegregation in academia hurt HBCUs, because top Black students left HBCUs and joined the White institutions for better academic, social acceptability and economic opportunities that are available in these institutions of higher learning. Prior to Brown's decision, Black students were forced to attend Black private and public institutions due to the law of segregation, except a few Northern institutions willing to admit Black students.

The flight of top Black students to HWI created an academic intellectual vacuum among Black colleges and universities, which resulted in an erosion of academic standards and intellectual productivity. Many capable faculty members left HBCUs to join HWI/ PWI at this point. The HBCUs were perceived by many Blacks as "inferior" to White institutions because a majority of high-achieving Black students abandoned their HBCUs.

CHAPTER 12

What HBCUs Need to Do to Survive in the Twenty-First Century

Historically black colleges and universities often receive negative media attention because of their financial troubles, mismanagement, accreditation problems, and low retention and graduation rates. Many question why there is a need for HBCUs when college admission is open for all if you qualify. Many argue that HBCUs are obsolete and nonfunctional academic institutions who served their role during post-slavery era. At present, no slavery exists today, so why keep doling out money to these institutions? Let them die!

The American public is brainwashed by the present political climate where there is a message trying to cover up that slavery was an institution to subjugate millions of African-Americans for centuries. That message is trying to tell that slavery no longer exists today and died a century ago. But suppression and control of human spirit, which was a part of the brutal ideology of slavery, has metamorphosed into new entities where poverty, segregation, inequity, and class separation can flourish.

History is the greatest chronicler of our existence. HBCUs are the part of American history we must uphold and cherish these institutions. If we neglect them, then we are trying to obliterate our own heritage and existence. The Black higher education started in the late nineteenth century, when in 1865 slavery was abolished, and the Freedmen Bureau with various churches created these institutions. Free slaves realized that to achieve real freedom, economic prosperity, and wealth, they had to receive an education that would allow them to attain their desired goal. In the spirit of achieving freedom, the freedmen put their minds into education, and within a short period surpassed the majority White population in every aspect of life.

Early twentieth century African-Americans achieved a well-to-do middle class who contributed a new Black culture, where arts, music, dance, and poetry created a golden era. Education played a very significant role in this golden era and the leaders who carried the torch of educational institutions were the Black intellectuals who believed in service and excellence. In the late twentieth century and early twenty-first century, the leadership of Black higher educational enterprise was somehow hijacked by a group of mediocre, anti-intellectuals who forgot the fundamentals of service and academic excellence for their clientele. Instead, they believed in their own personal economic gains and became a part of the entitlement generation. The lofty idealism of service for the people somehow got lost in the greed for power and capitalistic mentalities. This quick "cash in" ideology of the present academic leaders has destroyed the integrity and excellence of many institutions, and put them in the gutter where they are surrounded by poor academic outcomes, accreditation trouble, financial insolvency, plunging retention, and graduation rates and other problems.

Despite all these destructive conditions, the HBCUs have achieved almost impossible feats in their lifetime. HBCUs represent only 3 percent of all colleges and universities in the United States of America, and enroll over 11 percent Black post-secondary education student population; a majority of them are poor and first generation college student (Gasman 2013). HBCUs comprise a diverse group of institutions, mostly four-year institutions (87%). Fifty-one percent of them are public, 17% land-grant institutions, 23% awarded master's degree, 10% are research institutions, 2% medical schools, and 50% are private institutions.

HBCUs play an important role in science, technology, engineering, and mathematics sector in providing a large pool of well-qualified personnel who pursue careers in sciences, engineering, and physical sciences. Many of these trained personnel receive doctoral degrees that enhances American scientific and technical superiority over other countries through innovation and creativity. HBCUs produced 18% of all engineering degrees, 31% all biological science degrees, 31% of mathematics degree, 21% all business and management degrees, 42% all agricultural science degrees, and 17% all health profession degrees by African-American students in America (Historically Black Colleges and Universities HBCUs: a background primer, New America. n.d.).

A large middle class of well-educated African-Americans is the product of HBCUs and they are carrying the proud heritage within them. Because of a few greedy leaders among HBCUs who are dragging these institution to the ground for their own personal agenda and arrogant, dictatorial management policies, HBCUs must get rid of the so-called leaders and bring in new blood who are well-trained. HBCUs are well known for recycling failed leaders to run institutions. This policy should stop so that HBCUs can garner support from all corners and assure their competitiveness and survival.

Graduation rate in the majority of HBCUs is low for many reasons such as poor academic preparation, poverty, and other socio-economic shortcomings that influence academic achievement. Many concerned educators fail to point out a vital issue that is responsible for low graduation rate among HBCUs. This omission is perhaps intertwined with race that most educators avoid. The leadership of the majority of HBCUs representing small private institutions is guilty of perpetuating a cultural phenomenon coined as "retrograde culture." What is retrograde culture? The present student population belongs to "entitlement/you owe me generation" and practitioners of the "retrograde culture." This generation knows colleges need students to keep this business enterprise open, and the leadership supports students' demand for academic watered-down program/ curriculum, grade inflation, and many other anti-intellectual practices. Many students miss at least 15–20% of their class periods each semester, and when they are in the class they are glued to the cell phone/iPad and other devices texting/messaging and/or other social media activities. The professor providing instruction in the class only has twenty to thirty percent of their students listening, and the rest are busy doing their own things. If the teacher dared to ask a student to stop using a cell phone and answer the question she/he is seeking a response, the student would reply, "Why are you picking on me?" The teacher would stop probing further and move on to explain the answer to the question. If a student received an F or D grade for the course, the student could go to the dean and a request for "an appeal to change grades." The dean would make up a committee and the committee will evaluate the evidence and can recommend changing the grade. Before the committee meeting, the dean will remind all parties that retention of student is one of the most important duties of their work and they are working for the students.

All class assignments follow deadlines. In this retrograde culture, deadlines are unnecessary and never followed. In online courses, this deadline issue has reached a monumental failure. Many online professors complain that they have to change the deadlines for each assignment so often in a semester that many professors included the final day of the class as the deadline for all assignments.

To bump up the retention and better student rating professors are giving test review sheets before the final examination, and helping students in the tutorial sessions, so that all students can do well in the examination. Teachers are solving problems in sciences and other fields of studies for the students, rather than students learning how to solve analytical and thinking problems by themselves so that real learning can be achieved by the students. Students are retained and completing the undergraduate program and graduating within the six-year time frame designated by the federal government for receiving federal financial aids. This retrograde culture is destroying the academic honesty, integrity, and genuine learning at many HBCUs. Stop this "cultural tsunami" before the value and historic achievement of the HBCUs crashes down to oblivion.

American college graduates cannot compete internationally because they are not prepared enough. Chief executive officers (CEO) of many companies complain that half of the graduates cannot think critically, barely do the required jobs, have no creativity and innovative spirit, and are only interested in doing enough to get by with mediocrity. The military generals complain that our recruits cannot read and understand the safety manuals how to operate safely the sophisticated weaponry system. The clock is ticking! HBCUs need to reverse these self-inflicting damages so they can be competitive and vibrant academic institutions of higher learning again.

Governance

The board of trustees must be comprised of corporate leaders, educators, and a diverse group of professionals willing to maintain transparency and provide leadership that moves the institution forward. Their main role will be to provide a fiduciary responsibility and select a president who is well qualified, has knowledge and experience in running an academic sector, a polished and charming personality that attracts and exhibit the confidence of accomplishment, and acumen for openness and honesty. The board and the president must be open to the input of the faculty so that an open and free dialogue can transmit between these two parties. Academic institutions are standing on these three pillars—the board, the president, and faculty. As long as all parties believe in transparency, work as a team, and believe in accomplishment and greatness for the institution, then great achievements will follow.

The president's cabinet must include qualified personnel regardless of their political, sociological, and ethnic background. The main goal is to select capable people who could stand up and provide the best advice for the betterment and interest of the institution. Nepotism, favoritism, and Afro-centric ideological choices are not academic qualifications and should be avoided. The leadership must recognize that excellence and achievements are race neutral and colorless. The concept of role model and its value has been abused and practiced as a cover-up for racism. The actual meaning of role model means any person or group that provides exemplary leadership, accomplishes great things that enriches mankind, and creates an environment that elevates human consciousness and well-being. People like President Abraham Lincoln, Mahatma Gandhi, Martin Luther King Jr., Alexander Fleming, Albert Einstein, and others are the embodiment of role models because they represent the best humanity can offer, and they have no race, creed, color—just a member of *Homo sapiens.*

Accountability

The public suspects that higher educational enterprises are covering up their mismanagement and using tax dollars for their own personal gains. Most colleges provide limited resources for their clientele and are not doing enough to prepare their students for global competition. Public perception of the effectiveness of higher education is low. The higher educational enterprise must reverse this downward spiral of negative perception and elevate their effectiveness.

Philip L. Clay (2012) reported that to increase accountability, the institutions must use dashboard or other means of open communication where the institution would disclose how an institution operates, what kind of funding it is receiving, and other facts that would instill confidence in people that their tax dollars are used for better educational outcome. This accountability and transparency might cause problems for the leadership of the institution, but in the long run would allow a better and efficient operation of the institution.

Most HBCUs are located in the Southern States and are accredited by the Southern Association of Colleges and Schools (SACS). It is reported that from 1998 to 2013, SACS put twenty-nine HBCUs on warning and twenty on probation for not fulfilling the requirements for accreditation (Historically Black Colleges and Universities [HBCUs]; n.d.). HBCUs make up 13 percent of SACS membership but show 25 percent sanctions levied on them, showing many institutions are doing a very poor job in managing their institutions. Maintaining accreditation is essential because over 70 percent students receive federal financial aid dependent on the accreditation status. Institutions without accreditation have no financial aid from the federal government, and without support from the federal government, this institution cannot operate. Most private HBCUs are quasi-government institutions and dependent on the support from the government to keep the doors open for business.

Academic culture

HBCUs must work on the prevailing academic culture of each institution. The majority of private colleges do not have a healthy rigorous academic culture that demands a higher level of intellectualism, quest for knowledge, open-minded inquiry-based interaction, and free exchange of ideas between teachers and students. The lack of rigorous and mind-expanding themes prohibits students from dreaming the impossible dreams and seeing the limitless possibilities that lie ahead for them to attain and achieve.

Johnny Taylor, president and CEO of Thurgood Marshall College fund, said, "HBCUs admitting students reading on an eighth-grade level, taking thousands of dollars from them during their four or five or six years at college, and sending them out into the world not much better educated than when they arrived—in many cases, not even with the degree. That's the new black on black crime" (Stodghill 2015, 121).

If HBCUs graduates cannot keep a job or cannot compete because they are not prepared well by the college or university, then the blame should be on the academic institution that gave the degrees to these individuals. The graduates should blame the president of the university, the provost, the dean because they have produced a watered-down curriculum, lowered expectations, inflated the grades, and created an academic environment where mediocrity run supreme. Retrograde culture and "customers are always right" supported by the administration and muffled the voices of the faculty and made them impotent.

Many private HBCUs follow their tuition policies associated with the federal government grants and loan policies. If a Pell Grant increases the yearly appropriation, the college will increase the tuition according to the percentage point increment. The open admission policy allows a larger number of students to enroll in colleges, even if many of them are not prepared to take college-level rigorous courses but are assigned to remedial courses that do not count for college credits. These students drop out from the college within a year. Most college administrators know this trend, but they are instructed by the president of the college to admit these unprepared students, and take their money, which is unethical but the leadership feel that these unethical practices are acceptable in the business of academic enterprise. The college takes students' money but does not provide resources that would allow students to overcome their limitations and prepared to surmount challenges or obstacles. These retrograde cultures are flourishing in many private colleges among HBCUs.

Black students consider HBCU campuses during 1950 through 1990 as a place of reverence, and they worked very hard to achieve their educational and career goals. They thrived and demanded rigor and excellence. But the millennial generation who espouses entitlement mentality thinks colleges and universities are a place for fun, games, and enjoyment. The value system of academic rigor and excellence is absent in many campuses. The president and his/her entourage are interested in getting students' money so they can get their hefty paychecks and other perks that would fatten their coffer, but not at all interested to create college environment as a place for reverence and academic excellence. The net result of these anti-intellectualism that perpetuates retrograde culture in colleges and universities pushes many institutions into financial crisis, accreditation warning, probation, and other ailments including low retention, graduation, and higher default rates.

The survival of HBCUs depends on eliminating the retrograde culture and pseudo-intellectual leaders. If HBCUs can achieve these corrective surgical excisions of cancerous leadership, then educational excellence will be back in the campuses and will assure the survival of HBCUs. HBCUs survived and flourished during the era of Jim Crow, segregation, and brutal suppression. It can survive, thrive, and compete in the twenty-first century without a doubt. The government handout might come down to trickles; the ability, resilience, enthusiasm, hard work, and determination of students and faculty will keep the ship afloat in high menacing waves and in still water. Education is the salvation and force for real freedom.

The legacy of slavery in America created an environment that shackles and bonded the African-Americans for centuries. To break down that bondage, African-Americans need a new paradigm where education is the supreme force that would enlighten the mind and liberate the people. A new day will arrive and achieve real freedom.

In human history, all oppressors denied the oppressed the basic desire to be educated because they knew education has the power to topple their might of superiority. Education is the most powerful antidote against oppression. Ignorance, self-doubts, acquiescence, and hopelessness are the main fuel for the oppressor to use against his subjugated people so they could continue their abusive control and the domination. Education is the pathway for freedom, and African-Americans must forge ahead to achieve real freedom through educational attainment. African-Americans failed to take full advantage of education and the time is ripe to seize the power in their own hand so that a new destiny would be dawned.

Black higher education in America has yet to gain the desired results. It has failed to achieve the goals set by international academic standards. Leaders of Black educational enterprise always blame others for their failures, but they never took time to look at their own self and analyze the reasons for the shortcoming of the higher education they are leading. Majority of historically Black colleges and universities were created during the time of reconstruction era after the end of the Civil War. Free slaves were the most dedicated learners and determined to achieve the freedom through education, by developing skills and intellectual attainment. The freedmen were so dedicated for the quest of knowledge that poor Whites could not even fathom, so they had to resort to violence, intimidation, murder, brutality, and created the new government-sponsored rules and regulations to stop the Black educational progress. The attacks by Ku Klux Klan and establishment of Jim Crow law, peonage system, and segregation so that Black educational progress could stop. White oppressors knew educational attainment by Black Americans can stymie their power of dominance and in course of time, they will have no control over Black people.

The present generation of Black students is not serious about education. They are wasting their time and opportunities for upward mobility because they are not willing to achieve academic attainment. Education became a meaningless word to these "give me generation" youths who think they may get a college degree learning nothing. They demand that professors must give them good grades because they are paying for the college education. This is an outrageous mentality among a large section of college-bound Black students responsible for destroying the Black educational enterprise. Private colleges are supporting the new business model that dictates that "customers are always right and deserve best customer service." This model of operation has crippled the academic rigorousness and sanctity in most private institutions of higher learning today. Many leaders of private colleges and universities think the academic institution they are leading are for their own financial gain, and they abuse their power as the leader of the institution and give none importance to the lives of the younger generation they are supposed to help, and educate them.

This lack of commitment and seriousness is destroying the academic integrity and quality of many private HBCUs. To be competitive in the global arena, the HBCUs must develop a new strategy where the main thrust should be academic excellence through intense, rigorous, and challenging educational experiences to their student clientele that would prepare them for the challenges of tomorrow, which have yet to surface.

CHAPTER 13

Positive Epigenetic Influence Leads to Hope

Environmental conditions can influence our genetic makeup and can cause specific changes that alter the expression of our genes. DNA is a malleable molecule. It can change directly through mutation or by epigenetic means, where a series of chemical tags such as methyl groups are added or deleted, which modifies the DNA structure without altering genetic sequence along with histone proteins that can influence gene expression.

In rats the mother-pup contact occurs during a "nest-bout" when the mother gathers her litters and nurses them and frequently licks and grooms them until the mother leaves the nest. These licking/grooming and arched back nursing (LG-ABN) is a common maternal behavior during first week of lactation. Some mothers show more licking, grooming, and nursing behavior (high LG-ABN) than other group of mothers, who neglect the litters (low LG-ABN). Research revealed that pups who received high level of maternal care performed significantly better in spatial learning and memory during water maze experiments over pups who received poor maternal care. Cross-fostering studies revealed when low-high pups received care from a high LG-ABN mother, the pups showed spatial learning and memory similar like high LG-ABN pups reared by high LG-ABN mothers. In other words, better maternal care can reverse the effects of neglected mothering (Liu et al. 2000).

In mice the negative experiences such as absence of maternal grooming will epigenetically modify DNA methylation that would alter the glucocorticoid receptor expression and lead to higher levels of cortisol in the system (Plotsky and Meaney 1993).

In rats proper maternal care resulted in decreased methylation of the offspring. The Grm1 gene, which encodes metabotropic glutamate receptor (mGluR1), indicates epigenetic regulation of glutamatergic synaptic signaling that regulates hippocampal function and cognitive performance (Bagot et al. 2012).

Trauma and exposure to toxic stress in early life can cause various physiological, cognitive, and neurobehavioral problems, particularly in adult life (Klengel and Binder 2015). These effects can be transmitted to subsequent generations, even if their offspring were not exposed to trauma and toxic stress (Bohacek and Mansuy 2015). Often exposure to traumatic events and toxic stress leads to better coping abilities for these negative experiences (Franklin et al. 2012).

Exposure to most of these negative experiences affects the hypothalamic-pituitary-adrenal (HPA) axis that directly involves the glucocorticoid receptor (GR) and related biochemical partners such as cortisone that regulate the stress response system. It has been well established that GR gene activation or suppression influenced by environmental factors, as such associated with epigenetic regulation (Weaver et al. 2004).

Gapp and colleague (2016) reported that offspring of male mice exposed to traumatic and stressful experiences during early postnatal life develop a better appraisal and a greater ability to respond to adversity when they become adults. They also discovered that these cross-generational effects could be reversed if the fathers (male mice) were placed in an enriched environment. Then the sperm of adult fathers had increased DNA methylation (Gapp et al. 2016).

Epigenetic modification is directly influenced by the environmental factors. Negative experiences such as trauma, toxic stress, and other adversities can alter the DNA methylation/demethylation pattern, histone modification, and other epigenetic modifiers that could induce various pathophysiological, neurobiological and neurobehavioral manifestation in humans. It is quite possible to think that not all environmental factors would be negative/bad, but some may be positive, which will cause positive changes in epigenetic expression.

Gapp et al. (2016) showed that enriched environment helped mice to prevent transgenerational effects of paternal trauma. Rat pups born from uncaring mothers when placed under the care of a mother rat who showed high LG-ABN behavior developed higher spatial learning abilities. It is possible to reverse that damaging epigenetic modification in children through behavioral therapy such as hugging, cuddling, and other positive nurturing experiences that would reduce or eliminate the toxic stress (Kanherkar et al. 2014).

Most negative experiences are carried by poverty. Poverty leads to the most destructive force against normal growth and development of children. If poverty is eradicated, then almost all negative experiences in life will be vanished. Education has the power to eliminate poverty. If children in America receive an equitable share of positive environment, where they can grow up with less toxic stress exposure, and proper educational and mental nourishment through positive, caring teachers, and mentors, then they will exude positive energy that will change the epigenetic signature. In turn, this will allow better academic performance, positive health and mental attitude that would result in higher cognitive and executive functions. In other words, all these positive factors will lead to a better, healthy, intelligent, creative, and innovative person.

Education is the force, and it has the power to change all negativity in human lives. Let us nurture it!

REFERENCES

Adolphs, R., D. Tranel, H. Damasio, and A.R. Damasio. 1995. "Fear and the Human Amygdala." *Neurosci* 15: 5879–5891. doi:10.1093/neucas/3.4.267.

AAUP; n.d. Retrieved from: www.aaup.org

AGB Report; n.d. "Top Strategic Issues Facing HBCUs, Now and into the Future, AGB Report." Retrieved from: https://www.agb.org/sites/default/files/legacy/2014TopStrategicIssuesFacingH-BCUs.pdf. See also, https://www.agb.org/briefs/statementof-trustee-responsibility

Aggleton, John P., and Andrew W. Young. 2000. "The Enigma of the Amygdala. On Its Contribution to Human Emotion." In *Series in Affective Science*, edited by R.D. Lane and L. Nadel, 106–128. New York: Oxford University Press.

Agrawal, A. A. 2001. "Phenotypic Plasticity in the Interactions and Evolution of Species." *Science* 294 (5541): 321–326.

Alberts, Bruce, Alexander Johnson, Julian Lewis, Martin Raff, Keith Roberts, Peter Walter, and David Morgan. 2015. *Molecular Biology of the Cell.* 6th ed. New York: Garland Science.

Allen, T.W. 1994. *The Invention of the White Race.* Vol. 1. London and New York: Verso.

——— 1997. *The Invention of the White Race.* Vol. 2. London and New York: Verso.

Allis, C. David, Thomas Jenuwein, Danny Reinberg, and Marie-Laure Caparros. 2007. *Epigenetics.* New York: Cold Spring Harbor Laboratory Press.

Anderson, J.D. 1988. *The Education of Blacks in the South, 1860–1935.* Chapel Hill, NC: The University of North Carolina Press.

Armstrong, J.B. 2011. *Mary Turner and the Memory of Lynching.* Athens, GA: University of Georgia Press.

Arnsten, Amy F.T., Murray A. Raskind, Fletcher B. Taylor, and Daniel F. Connor. 2015. "The Effects of Stress Exposure on Prefrontal Cortex: Translating Basic Research into Successful Treatments for Post-Traumatic Stress Disorder." *Neurobiology of Stress* 1: 89–99. doi:10.1016/j.ynstr.2014.10.002.

Bagot, R. C., T.-Y. Zhang, X. Wen, T. T. T. Nguyen, H.-B. Nguyen, J. Diorio, T. P. Wong, and M. J. Meaney. 2012. "Variations in Postnatal Maternal Care and the Epigenetic Regulation of Metabotropic Glutamate Receptor 1 Expression and Hippocampal Function in the Rat." *Proceedings of the National Academy of Sciences* 109 (Supplement_2): 17200–17207.

Bahls, Steve C. 2014. "How to Make Shared Governance Work: Some Best Practices." AGB. https://www.agb.org/trusteeship/2014/3/how-make-shared-governance-work-some-best-practices.

Bahls, Steve. 2015. "What Is Shared Governance?." AGB. https://www.agb.org/blog/2015/12/22/what-is-shared-governance.

Baldwin, B., R. Moffet, and K. Lane. 1992. The High School Dropout: Antecedents, Societal Consequences and Alternatives. *Journal of School Leadership* 2: 355–362.

Balfanz, R., & Legters, N.E. 2004. "Locating the Dropout Crisis: Which High School Produce the Nation's Dropouts?." In *Dropouts in America: Confronting the Graduation Rate Crisis*, edited by G. Orfield, 57–84. Cambridge: Harvard Education Press.

Bamberger, Christoph M., Heinrich M. Schulte, and George P. Chrousos. 1996. "Molecular Determinants of Glucocorticoid Receptor Function and Tissue Sensitivity to Glucocorticoids." *Endocrine Reviews* 17 (3): 245–261.

Barker, D.J.P. 1995. "Fetal Origins of Adult Disease." Proc. Biol. Sci, 262, 37-43.

Baum, Andrew. 1990. "Stress, Intrusive Imagery, and Chronic Distress." *Health Psychology* 9 (6): 653–675.

Belfer, M.I. 2008. "Child and Adolescent Mental Disorders: The Magnitude of the Problem across the Globe." 49: 226–236.

Bennett, Lerone Jr. 1962. *Before the Mayflower: A History of the Negro in America 1619–1964*. Chicago: Johnson Publishing Company.

Berliner, David C. 2013. "Effects of Inequality and Poverty vs. Teachers and Schooling on America's Youth." *Teachers College Record* 115, 1–26.

Bernstein, Basil. 1971. "Class, Codes and Control, Volume I: Theoretical Studies towards a Sociology of Language." London: Routledge and Kegan Paul.

"Black Codes." *History*. http://www.history.com/topics/black-history/black-codes.

Black Chronology; n.d. Retrieved from: https://www.jbhe.com/chronology

Blair, Irene V. 2002. "The Malleability of Automatic Stereotypes and Prejudice." *Personality and Social Psychology Review* 6 (3).

Bohacek, Johannes, and Isabelle M. Mansuy. 2015. "Molecular Insights into Transgenerational Non-Genetic Inheritance of Acquired Behaviours." *Nature Reviews Genetics* 16 (11): 641–652.

Borman, G., and M. Dowling. 2010. "Schools and Inequality: A Multilevel Analysis of Coleman's Equality of Educational Opportunity Data." *Teachers College Record* 112 (5).

Bowdoin; n.d. Retrieved from: https://www.bowdoin.edu/president/governance/roles responsibilities.shtml

Bradley, Tashia Levanga. 2010. *The Race to Educate*. African American Resistance to Educational Segregation in Kentucky, 1885–1910. Ph.D dissertation. Tallahassee, Florida: Florida State University.

Breslau, Naomi. 1995. "Psychiatric Sequelae of Low Birth Weight." *Epidemiologic Reviews* 17 (1): 96–106.

Breslau, Naomi, Nancy Klein, and Lida Allen. 1988. "Very Low Birthweight: Behavioral Sequelae at Nine Years of Age." *Journal of the American Academy of Child and Adolescent Psychiatry* 27 (5): 605–612.

Brown, C. 1999. *The Quest to Define Collegiate Desegregation.* Black Colleges, Title VI compliance, and post-Adams litigation. Westport: Bergin & Garvey.

Buchanan, Ann, Joann Ten Brinke, and Eirini Flouri. 2000. "Parental Background, Social Disadvantage, Public 'Care,' and Psychological Problems in Adolescence and Adulthood." *Journal of the American Academy of Child and Adolescent Psychiatry* 39 (11): 1415–1423.

Bushnell, I.W.R. 2001. "Mother's Face Recognition in Newborn Infants: Learning and Memory." *Infant and Child Development* 10 (1–2): 67–74.

Caldji, C., B. Tannenbaum, S. Sharma, D. Francis, P. M. Plotsky, and M. J. Meaney. 1998. "Maternal Care During Infancy Regulates the Development of Neural Systems Mediating the Expression of Fearfulness in the Rat." *Proceedings of the National Academy of Sciences* 95 (9): 5335–5340.

Cardyn, Lisa. 2002. "Sexualized Racism/Gendered Violence: Outraging the Body Politic in the Reconstruction South." *Michigan Law Review* 100 (4); 675–867.

Carnoy, Martin, and Richard Rothstein. 2013. "What Do International Tests Show about US Student Performance? *Economic Policy Institute.* http://www.epi.org/publication/us-student-performance-testing/.

Carrasco, G.A., and L.D. Van de Kar,. 2003. "Neuroendocrine Pharmacology Of Stress." *Eur. J. Pharmacol,* no. 463: 235–272.

Cavalli-Sforza, Luigi Luca. 2000. *Genes, Peoples, and Languages.* Berkeley: University of California Press.

Cawthon, Richard M., Ken R. Smith, Elizabeth O'Brien, Anna Sivatchenko, and Richard A. Kerber. 2003. "Association between Telomere Length in Blood and Mortality in People Aged 60 Years or Older." *The Lancet* 361 (9355): 393–395.

Cervoni, Nadia, and Moshe Szyf. 2001. "Demethylase Activity Is Directed by Histone Acetylation." *Journal of Biological Chemistry* 276 (44): 40778–40787.

Chang, E., and C. B. Harley. 1995. "Telomere Length and Replicative Aging in Human Vascular Tissues." *Proceedings of the National*

Academy of Sciences 92 (24): 11190–11194. doi:10.1073/pnas.92.24.11190.

Chapman, Chris, Jennifer Laird, and Angelina KewalRamani. 2010. "Trends in High School Dropout and Completion Rates in the United States: 1972–2008." *National Center for Education Statistics*. https://nces.ed.gov/pubs2011/2011012.pdf.

Chen, Taiping, and En Li. 2004. "Structure and Function of Eukaryotic DNA Methyltransferases." *Current Topics in Developmental Biology* 60: 55–89.

Chen, Zhao-Xia, and Arthur D. Riggs. 2011. "DNA Methylation and Demethylation in Mammals." *Journal of Biological Chemistry* 286 (21): 18347–18353.

Cheyney University n.d. Retrieved from: www.cheyney.edu/about-cheyney-university/cheyney-history.cfm

Chwang, Wilson B., Kenneth J. O'Riordan, Jonathan M. Levenson, and J. David Sweatt. 2006. "ERK/MAPK Regulates Hippocampal Histone Phosphorylation Following Contextual Fear Conditioning." *Learning & Memory* 13 (3): 322–328.

Clay, P.L. 2012. Historically Black Colleges and Universities, Facing the Future: A Fresh Look at Challenges and Opportunities. Ebook. https://www.fordfoundation.org/media/1762/2012-facing-the-future.pdf.

Cohen, Sheldon, William J. Doyle, Ronald B. Turner, Cuneyt M. Alper, and David P. Skoner. 2004. "Childhood Socioeconomic Status and Host Resistance to Infectious Illness in Adulthood." *Psychosomatic Medicine* 66 (4): 553–558.

Cohen, S. B., M. E. Graham, G. O. Lovrecz, N. Bache, P. J. Robinson, and R. R. Reddel. 2007. "Protein Composition of Catalytically Active Human Telomerase from Immortal Cells." *Science* 315 (5820): 1850–1853.

Cohen, Sheldon, and Denise Janicki-Deverts. 2012. "Who's Stressed? Distributions of Psychological Stress in the United States in Probability Samples from 1983, 2006, and 20091." *Journal of Applied Social Psychology* 42 (6): 1320–1334.

Coleman, James S. 1966. *Equality of Educational Opportunity [Summary Report]*. Washington: U.S. Dept. of Health, Education, and Welfare, Office of Education.

Collins, Elizabeth M. 2013. "Black Soldiers in the Revolutionary War." *Soldiers Live.* https://www.army.mil/article/97705/black_soldiers_in_the_revolutionary_war.

Coley, Richard J., and Bruce Baker. 2013. *Poverty and Education: Finding the Way Forward,* ETS Report. www.ets.org/s/research/pdf/poverty_and_education_report.pdf

Condron, Dennis J. 2011. "Egalitarianism and Educational Excellence." *Educational Researcher* 40 (2): 47–55.

Correll, Joshua, Bernadette Park, Charles M. Judd, and Bernd Wittenbrink. 2002. "The Police Officer's Dilemma: Using Ethnicity to Disambiguate Potentially Threatening Individuals." *Journal of Personality and Social Psychology* 83 (6): 1314–1329.

Cottrell, Catherine A., and Steven L. Neuberg. 2005. "Different Emotional Reactions to Different Groups: A Sociofunctional Threat-Based Approach to 'Prejudice'." *Journal of Personality and Social Psychology* 88 (5): 770–789.

Danieli, Yael. 1998. *International Handbook of Multigenerational Legacies of Trauma*. New York: Plenum Press.

Dasgupta, N. 2009. "Mechanism Underlying the Malleability of Implicit Prejudice and Stereotypes: The Role of Automaticity and Cognitive Control. In *Handbook of Stereotyping, Prejudice, and Discrimination*, edited by T. Nelson, 267–284. New York, NY: Psychology Press

Davis, D. 2000. "Responsibilities of the College President." *Stchas. Edu.* https://www.stchas.edu/about-scc/administration/board-policies/112-Responsibilities-of-the-College-President.

DeBoer, Clara M. 1973. "Blacks and the American Missionary Association." *United Church of Christ.* http://www.ucc.org/about-us_hidden-histories_blacks-and-the-american

De Gruy, J. 2005. *Post Traumatic Slave Syndrome: America's Legacy of Enduring Injury and Healing*. Portland: Joy DeGruy Publications.

Denckla, M. B. 1994. "Measurement of Executive Function. In *Frames of Reference for the Assessment of Learning Disabilities: New Views on Measurement Issues*, edited by G. R. Lyon, 117–142. Baltimore: Paul H Brookes Publishing.

Deshpande, Manali S. 2010. "History of the Indian Caste System and Its Impact on India Today." San Luis Obispo Fall, CA: California Polythechnic State University. http://digitalcommons.calpoly.edu/cgi/viewcontent.cgi?article=1043&context=socssp

Dewey, John. 1916. *Democracy and Education*. New York: Free Press.

———. 1938. *Experience and Education*. New York: Macmillan. http://ruby.fgcu.edu/courses/ndemers/colloquium/experience-ducationdewey.pdf

Dias, Caroline, Jian Feng, Haosheng Sun, Ning yi Shao, Michelle S. Mazei-Robison, Diane Damez-Werno, and Kimberly Scobie et al. 2014. "Beta-Catenin Mediates Stress Resilience through Dicer1/MicroRNA Regulation." Nature 516: 51–55.

Ding, Jinlan, Fang Han, and Yuxiu Shi. 2010. "Single-Prolonged Stress Induces Apoptosis in the Amygdala in a Rat Model of Post-Traumatic Stress Disorder." *Journal of Psychiatric Research* 44 (1): 48–55.

Doll, Jonathan Jacob, Zohreh Eslami, and Lynne Walters. 2013. "Understanding Why Students Drop Out of High School, According to Their Own Reports." *SAGE Open* 3 (4): 215824401350383.

Drewe, E.A. 1974. "The Effect of Type and Area of Brain Lesion on Wisconsin Card Sorting Test Performance." *Cortex* 10 (2): 159–170.

Du Bois, W. E. B. 2007. *Dusk of Dawn: An Essay toward an Autobiography of a Race Concept*. New York: Oxford University Press.

Duggan, Maeve. 2013. "Cell Phone Activities 2013." *Pew Research Center: Internet, Science and Tech*. http://pewinternet.org/Reports/2013/Cell-Activities.aspx.

Dumont, Hanna, David Istance, and Francisco Benavides. 2010. *Nature of Learning*. Paris: Organisation for Economic Co-operation and Development.

Duncan, A. 2013. "The Threat of Educational Stagnation and Complacency: Remarks of US Secretary of Education Arne Duncan at the Release of the 2012 Program for PISA." http://www.ed.gov/news/speeches/threat-educational-stagnation-and-complacency.

Duster, Troy. 2009. "The Long Path to Higher Education for African Americans. *NEA Higher Education Journal,* 99–110. http://www.nea.org/assets/docs/HE/TA09PathHEDuster.pdf

Eberhardt, J.L., P.A. Goff, V.J. Purdie, and P.G. Davies. 2004. "Seeing Black: Race, Crime, and Visual Processing." *Journal of Personality and Social Psychology* 87 (6): 876–893.

Education Week. 2012. *Diplomas Count 2012: Trailing Behind, Moving Forward: Latino Students in U.S. Schools.* Washington, DC: Education Week. http://www.edweek.org/ew/toc/2012/06/07/.

Elston, Guy N., Ruth Benavides-Piccione, Alejandra Elston, Bendan Zietsch, Javier Defelipe, Paul Manger, Vivien Casagrande, and Jon H. Kaas. 2005. "Specializations of the Granular Prefrontal Cortex of Primates: Implications for Cognitive Processing." *The Anatomical Record Part A: Discoveries in Molecular, Cellular, and Evolutionary Biology* 288A (1): 26–35.

Epel, E. S., E. H. Blackburn, J. Lin, F. S. Dhabhar, N. E. Adler, J. D. Morrow, and R. M. Cawthon. 2004. "Accelerated Telomere Shortening in Response to Life Stress." *Proceedings of the National Academy of Sciences* 101 (49): 17312–17315.

Epel, Elissa S. 2009. "Telomeres in a Life-Span Perspective." *Current Directions in Psychological Science* 18 (1): 6–10.

Equal Justice Initiative. 2017. *Lynching in America: Confronting the Legacy of Racial Terror.* https://lynchinginamerica.eji.org/drupal/sites/default/files/2017-07/lynching-in-america-3d-edition-spread.pdf.

"Fast Facts - Historically Black Colleges and Universities." 2018. *National Center for Education Statistics.* https://nces.ed.gov/fastfacts/display.asp?id=667.

Fazio, Russell H., Joni R. Jackson, Bridget C. Dunton, and Carol J. Williams. 1995. "Variability in Automatic Activation as an Unobtrusive Measure of Racial Attitudes: A Bona Fide Pipeline?." *Journal of Personality and Social Psychology* 69 (6): 1013–1027. doi:10.1037/0022-3514.69.6.1013.

Finkelman, P. 2012. "Slavery in the United States: Persons or Property?." In *The Legal Understanding of Slavery: From the Historical to the Contemporary*, edited by J. Allain, 105–134. Oxford: Oxford University Press. https://scholarship.law.duke.edu/viewcontent. cgi?article=5386&context=faculty-scholarship.

Fischer, Andre, Farahnaz Sananbenesi, Xinyu Wang, Matthew Dobbin, and Li-Huei Tsai. 2007. "Recovery of Learning and Memory Is Associated with Chromatin Remodeling." *Nature* 447 (7141): 178–182.

Fleischman, H.L, P.J. Hopstock, M.P. Pelezar, and B.E. Shelley. 2010. *Highlights from PISA 2009 Performance Of U.S. 15-Year-Old Students in Reading, Mathematics, and Science Literacy in an International Context*. Washington, DC: National Center for Education Statistics, Institute of Education Sciences, U.S. Dept. of Education.

Fleming, A.S., D.H. O'Day, and G.W. Kraemer. 1999. "Neurobiology of Mother–Infant Interactions: Experience and Central Nervous System Plasticity across Development and Generations." *Neuroscience & Biobehavioral Reviews* 23 (5): 673–685.

Fletcher, P. 1998. "The Functional Roles of Prefrontal Cortex in Episodic Memory. I. Encoding." *Brain* 121 (7): 1239–1248.

Forbes List; n.d. Retrieved from: https://www.forbes.com/colleges/ howard-university/

Franics, Darlene D., Frances A. Champagne, Dong Liu, and Michael J. Meaney. 1999. "Maternal Care, Gene Expression, and the Development of Individual Differences in Stress Reactivity." *Annals of the New York Academy of Sciences* 896 (1): 66–84.

Franklin, Tamara B., Bechara J. Saab, and Isabelle M. Mansuy. 2012. "Neural Mechanisms of Stress Resilience and Vulnerability." *Neuron* 75 (5): 747–761.

Fredrickson, George M. 1988. *The Arrogance of Race*. Middletown, Conn.: Wesleyan University Press.

———. 2002. *Racism: A Short History*. Princeton, NJ: Princeton University Press.

Frodl, Thomas, Eva Maria Meisenzahl, Thomas Zetzsche, Christine Born, Markus Jäger, Constanze Groll, Ronald Bottlender, Gerda Leinsinger, and Hans-Jürgen Möller. 2003. "Larger Amygdala Volumes in First Depressive Episode As Compared to Recurrent Major Depression and Healthy Control Subjects." *Biological Psychiatry* 53 (4): 338–344.

Fromm, E. 2018. *To Have or to Be*. London: Abacus.

Gapp, Katharina, Johannes Bohacek, Jonas Grossmann, Andrea M Brunner, Francesca Manuella, Paolo Nanni, and Isabelle M Mansuy. 2016. "Potential of Environmental Enrichment to Prevent Transgenerational Effects of Paternal Trauma." *Neurops ychopharmacology* 41 (11): 2749–2758.

Gardner, Michael, David Bann, Laura Wiley, Rachel Cooper, Rebecca Hardy, Dorothea Nitsch, and Carmen Martin-Ruiz et al. 2014. "Gender and Telomere Length: Systematic Review and Meta-Analysis." *Experimental Gerontology* 51: 15–27.

Gasman, Marybeth, and Adriel A. Hilton. 2010. "A 25-Year History of the American Association of University Professors' Perspective on Shared Governance at Historically Black Colleges and Universities." *Journal of Research in Education* 20 (1): 53–60. http://www.adrielhilton.com/wp-content/uploads/2013/04/A-25-year-History-of-the-American-Association-of-University-Professors-perspective-on-shared-Governance-at-HBCUs.pdf.

Gasman, Marybeth. 2013. "The Changing Facts of Historically Black Colleges and Universities." http://www.gse.upenn.edu/Pdf/cmsi/Changing_Face_HBCUs.pdf.

Gavory, G. 2002. "Minimum Length Requirement of the Alignment Domain of Human Telomerase RNA to Sustain Catalytic Activity In Vitro." *Nucleic Acids Research* 30 (20): 4470–4480.

Geronimus, Arline T., Margaret T. Hicken, Jay A. Pearson, Sarah J. Seashols, Kelly L. Brown, and Tracey Dawson Cruz. 2010.

"Do US Black Women Experience Stress-Related Accelerated Biological Aging?." *Human Nature* 21 (1): 19–38.

Gieg, S. 2015–2016. "Using Knowledge of the Brain to Address Racism of College Students." *Journal of the Student Personnel Association at Indiana University,* 63–70. https://education. indiana.edu/graduate/programs/hesa/iuspa/2016%20SPA%20 at%20IU%20Journal.pdf.

Gluckman, P. D., M. A. Hanson, and T. Buklijas. 2009. "A Conceptual Framework for the Developmental Origins of Health and Disease." *Journal of Developmental Origins of Health and Disease* 1 (01): 6–18.

Goldberg, Aaron D., C. David Allis, and Emily Bernstein. 2007. "Epigenetics: A Landscape Takes Shape." *Cell* 128 (4): 635–638.

Goldfine, A. 2001. "Adrenal Medulla." In *Basic and Clinical Endocrinology*, edited by F.S.Greenspan and D.G. Gardner, 399–421. Lange Medical Books, McGraw Hill as cited in Padgett & Glaser 2003.

Goll, Mary Grace, and Timothy H. Bestor. 2005. "Eukaryotic Cytosine Methyltransferases." *Annual Review of Biochemistry* 74 (1): 481–514.

Gonzales, P., L. Jocelyn, S. Roey, D. Katberg, S. Brenwald, and T. Williams. 2008. *Highlights from TIMSS 2007Mathematics and Science Achievement of US Fourth- and Eighth-Grade Students in an International Context.* Washington, DC: National Center for Education Statistics, Institute of Education Sciences, U.S. Dept. of Education.

Goodman, Sherryl H., and Ian H. Gotlieb. 1999. "Risk for Psychopathology in the Children of Depressed Mothers: A Developmental Model for Understanding Mechanisms of Transmission." *Psychological Review* 106 (3): 458–490.

Gotlieb, I. H., J. LeMoult, N. L. Colich, L. C. Foland-Ross, J. Hallmayer, J. Joormann, J. Lin, and O. M. Wolkowitz. 2015. "Telomere Length and Cortisol Reactivity in Children of Depressed Mothers." *Molecular Psychiatry* 20 (5): 615–620.

Gräff, Johannes, Dohoon Kim, Matthew M. Dobbin, and Li-Huei Tsai. 2011. "Epigenetic Regulation of Gene Expression in

Physiological and Pathological Brain Processes." *Physiological Reviews* 91 (2): 603–649.

Greenwald, Anthony G., and Mahzarin R. Banaji. 1995. "Implicit Social Cognition: Attitudes, Self-Esteem, and Stereotypes." *Psychological Review* 102 (1): 4–27.

Grinnell, R. 2016. "Implicit Attitude." *Psych Central.* https://psych-central.com/encyclopedia/implicit-attitude/.

Hack, Maureen, Daniel J. Flannery, Mark Schluchter, Lydia Cartar, Elaine Borawski, and Nancy Klein. 2002. "Outcomes in Young Adulthood for Very-Low-Birth-Weight Infants." *New England Journal of Medicine* 346 (3), 149- 157.

Haller, J.S.Jr. 1971. *Outcasts from Evolution: Scientific Attitudes of Racial Inferiority, 1859–1900.* Urbana: University of Illinois Press.

Hanson, J.L., B. Nacewicz, M.J. Sutterer, A.A. Cayo, S.M. Schaefer, K.D. Rudolph, E.A. Shirtcliff, S.D. Pollak, and R.J. Davidson. 2015. "Behavioral Problems after Early Life Stress: Contributions of the Hippocampus and Amygdala." *Biological Psychiatry,* 77: 314–323.

Hanushek, E.A., P.E. Peterson, and L. Woessmann. 2014. "Not Just the Problems of Other People's Children: US Student Performance in Global Perspective. *Harvard's Program on Education Policy and Governance and Education Next.* http://www.hks.harvard.edu/pepg/PDF/Papers/PEPG14_01_NotJust.pdf.

Hart, Allen J., Paul J. Whalen, Lisa M. Shin, Sean C. McInerney, Håkan Fischer, and Scott L. Rauch. 2000. "Differential Response in the Human Amygdala to Racial Outgroup vs. Ingroup Face Stimuli." *Neuroreport* 11 (11): 2351–2354.

Haussmann, Mark F., and Britt J. Heidinger. 2015. "Telomere Dynamics May Link Stress Exposure and Ageing across Generations." *Biology Letters* 11 (11): 20150396.

Herman, James P., Michelle M. Ostrander, Nancy K. Mueller, and Helmer Figueiredo. 2005. "Limbic System Mechanisms of Stress Regulation: Hypothalamo-Pituitary-Adrenocortical Axis." *Progress in Neuro-Psychopharmacology and Biological Psychiatry* 29 (8): 1201–1213.

"Historically Black Colleges and Universities (HBCUs): A Background Primer." 2015. *New America.* https://www.newamerica.org/post-secondary-national-policy-institute/our-blog/historically-black-colleges-and-universities-hbcus/.

History.Com; n.d. Retrieved from www.history.com/topics/black-history/freedmens-bureau/

History.com; n.d, Andrew Johnson. Retrieved from: http://www.history.com/topics/us-presidents/andrew-johnson. See also, History.com; n.d. Retrieved from https://www.history.com/topics/black-history/plessy-v-ferguson.

"How Common Is PTSD? - PTSD: National Center For PTSD." n.d. *U.S. Department of Veteran Affairs.* https://www.PtsD.Va.gov/Public/PtsD-overview/basics/how-common-is-ptsd.asp.

Howlett, Sarah K., and Wolf Reik. 1991. "Methylation Levels of Maternal and Paternal Genomes During Pre-Implantation Development." *Development* 113 (1): 119–127.

Huffman, Kenneth E., Stephen D. Levene, Valerie M. Tesmer, Jerry W. Shay, and Woodring E. Wright. 2000. "Telomere Shortening Is Proportional to the Size of the G-Rich Telomeric 3'-Overhang." *Journal of Biological Chemistry* 275 (26): 19719–19722.

Hutvagner, György, Juanita McLachlan, Amy E. Pasquinelli, Eva Bálint, Thomas Tuschl, and Phillip D. Zamore. 2001. "A Cellular Function for the RNA-Interference Enzyme Dicer in the Maturation of the let-7 Small Temporal RNA." *Science* 293 (5531): 834–838.

Isenberg, Nancy. 2016. *White Trash: The 400-Year Untold History of Class in America.* New York: Viking.

Issler, Orna, and Alon Chen. 2015. "Determining the Role of MicroRNAs in Psychiatric Disorders." *Nature Reviews Neuroscience* 16 (4): 201–212.

Jackson, P.W. 2012. *What Is Education?.* Chicago: University of Chicago Press.

Jacobson, Lauren, and Robert Sapolsky. 1991. "The Role of the Hippocampus in Feedback Regulation of the Hypothalamic-Pituitary-Adrenocortical Axis." *Endocrine Reviews* 12 (2): 118–134.

Jennings, B.J., S.E. Ozanne, M.W. Dorling, and C.N. Hales. 1999. "Early Growth Determines Longevity in Male Rats and May Be Related to Telomere Shortening in the Kidney." *FEBS Letters* 448 (1): 4–8.

Jargowsky, P., and M. El Komi. 2011. "Before or after the Bell? School Context and Neighborhood Effects on Student Achievement. In *Neighborhood and Life Chances: How Place Matters in Modern America*, edited by H.B. Newburger, E.L. Birch, and S.M. Wachter, 50–72. Philadelphia: University of Pennsylvania Press.

Jarmusz, Tony S. 2018. "B-CU Nursing Program Slapped with Probation." Daytona Beach News-Journal. http://www.news-journalonline.com/news/20180208/b-cu-nursing-program-slapped-with-probation.

Jayaram, V. n.d. Hinduism and Caste System. *Hinduwebsite.com.* http://www.hinduwebsite.com/hinduism/h_caste.asp

Johnson, Andrew. 1867. "Third Annual Message to Congress." *The American Presidency Project.* http://www.presidency.ucsb.edu/ws/?pid=29508.

Johnson, A. 2013. *Cell and Molecular Biology: Concepts and Experiments.* 7th ed. Hoboken, NJ: John Wiley and Sons.

Jordan, Will J., Julia Lara, and James M. Mcpartland. 1994. "Exploring the Complexity of Early Dropout Casual Structures. Baltimore, MD: Center for Research on Effective Schooling for Disadvantaged Students." *Youth and Society.* The John Hopkins University.

Joughin, Louis. 1969. Academic Freedom and Tenure: A Handbook of the American Association of University Professors. Ed. L. Joughin. Madison: University of Wisconsin Press.

Kadonaga, James T. 1998. "Eukaryotic Transcription: An Interlaced Network of Transcription Factors and Chromatin-Modifying Machines." *Cell* 92 (3): 307–313.

Kanherkar, Riya R., Naina Bhatia-Dey, and Antonei B. Csoka. 2014. "Epigenetics across the Human Lifespan." *Frontiers in Cell and Developmental Biology* 2: 48.

Karp, Gerald. 2013. *Cell and Molecular Biology: Concepts and Experiments.* 7th ed. Hoboken, NJ: John Wiley and Sons.

Kelly, Y.J., J.Y Nazroo, A. McMunn, R. Boreham, and M. Marmot. 2001. "Birth Weight and Behavioral Problems in Children: A Modifiable Effect." *International Journal of Epidemiology*, 30: 88–91.

Kessler, Ronald C., Patricia Berglund, Olga Demler, Robert Jin, Kathleen R. Merikangas, and Ellen E. Walters. 2005. "Lifetime Prevalence and Age-of-Onset Distributions of DSM-IV Disorders in the National Comorbidity Survey Replication." *Archives of General Psychiatry* 62 (6): 593–602.

Kim, Jieun E., In Kyoon Lyoo, Annette M. Estes, Perry F. Renshaw, Dennis W. Shaw, Seth D. Friedman, Dajung J. Kim, Sujung J. Yoon, Jaeuk Hwang, and Stephen R. Dager. 2010. "Laterobasal Amygdalar Enlargement in 6- to 7-Year-Old Children with Autism Spectrum Disorder." *Archives of General Psychiatry* 67 (11); 1187–1197.

Klengel, Torsten, Divya Mehta, Christoph Anacker, Monika Rex-Haffner, Jens C Pruessner, Carmine M Pariante, and Thaddeus W W Pace et al. 2012. "Allele-Specific FKBP5 DNA Demethylation Mediates Gene–Childhood Trauma Interactions." *Nature Neuroscience* 16 (1): 33–41.

Klengel, Torsten, and Elisabeth B. Binder. 2015. "Epigenetics of Stress-Related Psychiatric Disorders and Gene × Environment Interactions." *Neuron* 86 (6): 1343–1357.

Kornberg, R. D. 1974. "Chromatin Structure: A Repeating Unit of Histones and DNA." *Science* 184 (4139): 868–871.

Kubota, J.T., M.R. Banaji, and E.A Phelps. 2012. "The Neuroscience of Race." *Nature Neuroscience* 15 (7): 940–948.

LaBar, Kevin S., and Roberto Cabeza. 2006. "Cognitive Neuroscience of Emotional Memory." *Nature Reviews Neuroscience* 7 (1): 54–64.

Labonté, Benoit, Matt Suderman, Gilles Maussion, Luis Navaro, Volodymyr Yerko, Ian Mahar, and Alexandre Bureau et al. 2012. "Genome-Wide Epigenetic Regulation by Early-Life Trauma." *Archives Of General Psychiatry* 69 (7): 722–731.

Laccarino, A. n d. "The Founding Fathers and Slavery." *Encyclopedia Britannica Online.* https://www.britannica.com/topic/the-founding-fathers-and-slavery-1269536.

Ladenburg, T. n.d. "Methods of Controlling Slaves." *Digital History.* http://www.digitalhistory.uh.edu/teachers/lesson_plans/pdfs/unit4_5.pdf

Leary, Joy DeGruy. 2005. *Post Traumatic Slave Syndrome: America's Legacy of Enduring Injury and Healing.* Portland: Joy DeGruy Publications.

LeDoux, J. 2002. *Synaptic Self: How Our Brains Become Who We Are.* New York: Viking Penguin.

LeDoux, J.E. 2015. *Anxious: Using the Brain to Understand and Treat Fear and Anxiety.* New York: Viking.

Levenson, Jonathan M., Kenneth J. O'Riordan, Karen D. Brown, Mimi A. Trinh, David L. Molfese, and J. David Sweatt. 2004. "Regulation of Histone Acetylation During Memory Formation in the Hippocampus." *Journal Of Biological Chemistry* 279 (39): 40545-40559.

Levenson, Jonathan M., Tania L. Roth, Farah D. Lubin, Courtney A. Miller, I-Chia Huang, Priyanka Desai, Lauren M. Malone, and J. David Sweatt. 2006. "Evidence That DNA (Cytosine-5) Methyltransferase Regulates Synaptic Plasticity in the Hippocampus." *Journal Of Biological Chemistry* 281 (23): 15763–15773.

Levin, H.M., and C.R. Belfield. 2007. "Educational Interventions to Raise High School Graduation Rates." In *The Price We Pay: Economic and Social Consequences of Inadequate Education,* edited by C.R. Belfield and H.M. Levin, 177–199. Washington, DC: Brookings Institution, as cited in Stark and Noel 2015.

Levine, S. 1994. "The Ontogeny of the Hypothalamic-Pituitary-Adrenal Axis. The Influence of Maternal Factors." *Annals of the New York Academy of Sciences* 746: 275–293.

Lewis, Andrew J. 2012. "A Call for an Expanded Synthesis of Developmental and Evolutionary Paradigms." *Behavioral and Brain Sciences* 35 (05): 368–369.

Lewis, Andrew James, Megan Galbally, Tara Gannon, and Christos Symeonides. 2014. "Early Life Programming As a Target for Prevention of Child and Adolescent Mental Disorders." *BMC Medicine* 12 (1), 33.

Lewontin, R. C. 1972. "The Apportionment of Human Diversity." In *Evolutionary Biology*, 6, 381–398, edited by T. Dobzhansky, M.K. Hecht, and W.C. Steere. New York, NY: Appleton-Century-Crofts.

Lieberman, M.D., A. Hariri, J.M. Jarcho, N.I. Eisenberger, and S.Y. Bookheimer. 2018. "An fMRI Investigation of Race-Related Amygdala Activity in African-American and Caucasian-American Individuals." *Nature Neuroscience*, 8: 720–722.

Lingner, J., and T. R. Cech. 1996. "Purification of Telomerase from Euplotes Aediculatus: Requirement of a Primer 3' Overhang." *Proceedings of the National Academy of Sciences* 93 (20): 10712–10717.

Liu, Dong, Josie Diorio, Beth Tannenbaum, Christian Caldji, Darlene Francis, Alison Freedman, Shakti Sharma, Deborah Pearson, Paul M. Plotsky, and Micheal J. Meaney. 1997. "Maternal Care, Hippocampal Glucocorticoid Receptors, and Hypothalamic-Pituitary-Adrenal Responses to Stress." *Science* 277 (5332): 1659–1662.

Liu, Dong, Josie Diorio, Jamie C. Day, Darlene D. Francis, and Michael J. Meaney. 2000. "Maternal Care, Hippocampal Synaptogenesis and Cognitive Development in Rats." *Nature Neuroscience* 3 (8): 799–806.

Livingstone, R. 1953. "What Is Education?." *British Medical Journal*, 2 (4834): 454–456.

Loury, Glenn C. 1998. "An American Tragedy: The Legacy of Slavery Lingers in Our Cities' Ghettos." *Brookings*. https://www. brookings.edu/articles/an-american-tragedy-the-legacy-of-slavery-lingers-in-our-cities-ghettos/

Lubin, F. D., T. L. Roth, and J. D. Sweatt. 2008. "Epigenetic Regulation of Bdnf Gene Transcription in the Consolidation of Fear Memory." *Journal of Neuroscience* 28 (42): 10576–10586.

Luria, Aleksandr Romanovich. 1966. *Higher Cortical Functions in Man*. New York: Basic Books.

MacQuarrie, J. 1978. *Christian Hope*. Oxford: Mowbray, as cited in Smith 2015, 11.

Malan, Stefanie, Sian Hemmings, Martin Kidd, Lindi Martin, and Soraya Seedat. 2011. "Investigation of Telomere Length and Psychological Stress in Rape Victims." *Depression and Anxiety* 28 (12): 1081–1085.

Maner, Jon K., Douglas T. Kenrick, D. Vaughn Becker, Theresa E. Robertson, Brian Hofer, Steven L. Neuberg, Andrew W. Delton, Jonathan Butner, and Mark Schaller. 2005. "Functional Projection: How Fundamental Social Motives Can Bias Interpersonal Perception." *Journal of Personality and Social Psychology* 88 (1): 63–78.

Matheson, G. Keith, B.J. Branch, and A. Newman Taylor. 1971. "Effects of Amygdaloid Stimulation on Pituitary-Adrenal Activity in Conscious Cats." *Brain Research* 32 (1): 151–167.

Mathur, Maya B., Elissa Epel, Shelley Kind, Manisha Desai, Christine G. Parks, Dale P. Sandler, and Nayer Khazeni. 2016. "Perceived Stress and Telomere Length: A Systematic Review, Meta-Analysis, and Methodologic Considerations for Advancing the Field." *Brain, Behavior, and Immunity* 54: 158–169.

McCorry, L.K. 2007. "Physiology of the Autonomic Nervous System." *American Journal of Pharmaceutical Education* 71 (4); Article 78.

McEwen, Bruce S. 1998. "Protective and Damaging Effects of Stress Mediators." *New England Journal of Medicine* 338 (3): 171–179.

McEwen, Bruce S. 2003. "Mood Disorders and Allostatic Load." *Biol Psychiatry* 54, 200-207.

———. 2005. "Glucocorticoids, Depression, and Mood Disorders: Structural Remodeling in the Brain." *Metabolism* 54 (5): 20–23.

McGowan, Patrick O, Aya Sasaki, Ana C D'Alessio, Sergiy Dymov, Benoit Labonté, Moshe Szyf, Gustavo Turecki, and Michael J Meaney. 2009. "Epigenetic Regulation of the Glucocorticoid Receptor in Human Brain Associates with Childhood Abuse." *Nature Neuroscience* 12 (3): 342–348.

McMillen, M., P. Kaufman, E. Hausken, and D. Brady. 1993. "Dropout Rates in the United States: 1992. Washington, DC: National Center for Education Statistics, Office of Educational Research and Improvement, U.S. Department of Education, as cited by Doll et al. 2013.

Meaney, Michael J. 2001. "Maternal Care, Gene Expression, and the Transmission of Individual Differences in Stress Reactivity across Generations." *Annual Review of Neuroscience* 24 (1): 1161–1192.

Meerson, Ari, Luisa Cacheaux, Ki Ann Goosens, Robert M. Sapolsky, Hermona Soreq, and Daniela Kaufer. 2010. "Changes in Brain MicroRNAs Contribute to Cholinergic Stress Reactions." *Journal of Molecular Neuroscience* 40 (1–2): 47–55.

Merriam-Webster, n.d. Retrieved from: https://www.merriam-web-ster.com/dictionary/racism

Mickelson, R.A. 2018. "Segregation and the SAT." *Ohio State Law Journal*, no. 67: 157–200.

Mitra, R., S. Jadhav, B. S. McEwen, A. Vyas, and S. Chattarji. 2005. "Stress Duration Modulates the Spatiotemporal Patterns of Spine Formation in the Basolateral Amygdala." *Proceedings of the National Academy of Sciences* 102 (26): 9371–9376.

Miller, Courtney A., and J. David Sweatt. 2007. "Covalent Modification of DNA Regulates Memory Formation." *Neuron* 53 (6): 857–869.

Miller, Courtney A., Susan L. Campbell, and J. David Sweatt. 2008. "DNA Methylation and Histone Acetylation Work in Concert to Regulate Memory Formation and Synaptic Plasticity." *Neurobiology of Learning and Memory* 89 (4): 599–603.

Miller, B. 2017. "New Federal Data Show a Student Loan Crisis for African-American Borrowers." *Center for American Progress.* https://www.americanprogress.org/issues/education-postsec-ondary/news/2017/10/16/440711/new-federal-data-show-stu-dent-loan-crisis-african-american-borrowers/.

Miranda, Tina Branscombe, and Peter A. Jones. 2007. "DNA Methylation: The Nuts and Bolts of Repression." *Journal Of Cellular Physiology* 213 (2): 384–390.

Monk, Marilyn, Micheal Boubelik, and Sigrid Lehnert. 1987. "Temporal and Regional Changes in DNA Methylation in the Embryonic, Extraembryonic and Germ Cell Lineages during Mouse Embryo Development." *Development* 99 (3): 371–382.

Morgan, Edmund S. 1975. *American Slavery, American Freedom.* New York: Norton.

Morrill Acts of 1862 and 1890; n.d. Retrieved from: www.1890universities.org/history. Also, Morrill Acts- lawhigheredu.com/90-morrill-acts.html

Mosconi, Matthew W., Heather Cody-Hazlett, Michele D. Poe, Guido Gerig, Rachel Gimpel-Smith, and Joseph Piven. 2009. "Longitudinal Study of Amygdala Volume and Joint Attention in 2- to 4-Year-Old Children with Autism." *Archives of General Psychiatry* 66 (5): 509.

Moss, N. 2018. "The Body Politics and Power of Socio-Economic Status." *American Journal Public of Health*, no. 87: 1411–1413.

Mukhopadhyay, Carol Chapnick, Rosemary C Henze, and Yolanda T Moses. 2014. *How Real Is Race? A Sourcebook on Race, Culture, and Biology.* 2nd ed. Lanham, MD: Rowman & Littlefield.

Murgatroyd, Chris, Alexandre V Patchev, Yonghe Wu, Vincenzo Micale, Yvonne Bockmühl, Dieter Fischer, Florian Holsboer, Carsten T Wotjak, Osborne F X Almeida, and Dietmar Spengler. 2009. "Dynamic DNA Methylation Programs Persistent Adverse Effects of Early-Life Stress." *Nature Neuroscience* 12 (12): 1559–1566.

National Center for PTSD; n.d. Retrieved from: https://www.PtsD.Va.gov/Public/PtsD-overview/basics/how-common-is-ptsd.asp

National Commission on Excellence in Education. "A Nation at Risk: The Imperative for Educational Reform." 1983. https://www.edreform.com/wp-content/uploads/2013/02/A_Nation_At_Risk_1983.pdf.

National Scientific Council on the Developing Child 2005/2014. "Excessive Stress Disrupts the Architecture of the Developing Brain." www. developingchild.harvard.edu.

Nature Index, n.d. Retrieved from: https://www.natureindex.com/institution-outputs/united-states-of-america-usa/howarduniversity/513906bd34d6b65e6a0004c8;https://www.natureindex.com/annualtables/2016/institution/academic/all/countries- United%20States%20of%20America %20%28USA%29

NCES Fast Facts; n.d. Retrieved from https://nces.ed.gov/fastfacts/display.asp?id=667

Nelson, J. 1990. "Mo' Better Spike." *Essence*, 55.

Northup, S. 2014. *12 Years a Slave: A True Story*. London: HarperCollins Publishers.

Nosek, Brian A., Frederick L. Smyth, Jeffrey J. Hansen, Thierry Devos, Nicole M. Lindner, Kate A. Ranganath, and Colin Tucker Smith et al. 2007. "Pervasiveness and Correlates of Implicit Attitudes and Stereotypes." *European Review of Social Psychology* 18 (1): 36–88.

Nosek, B.A., A.G. Greenwald, and M.R. Banaji. 2007. "The Implicit Association Test at Age 7: A Methodological and Conceptual Review." In *Automatic Processes in Social Thinking and Behavior*, edited by J.A. Bargh, 265–292. Psychological Press.

O'Donovan, Aoife, Elissa Epel, Jue Lin, Owen Wolkowitz, Beth Cohen, Shira Maguen, Thomas Metzler, Maryann Lenoci, Elizabeth Blackburn, and Thomas C. Neylan. 2011. "Childhood Trauma Associated with Short Leukocyte Telomere Length in Posttraumatic Stress Disorder." *Biological Psychiatry* 70 (5): 465–471.

O'Sullivan, Roderick J., and Jan Karlseder. 2010. "Telomeres: Protecting Chromosomes against Genome Instability." *Nature Reviews Molecular Cell Biology* 11 (3): 171–181.

Oh, H., S. C. Wang, A. Prahash, M. Sano, C. S. Moravec, G. E. Taffet, L. H. Michael, K. A. Youker, M. L. Entman, and M. D. Schneider. 2003. "Telomere Attrition and Chk2 Activation in Human Heart Failure." *Proceedings of the National Academy of Sciences* 100 (9): 5378–5383.

Okano, Masaki, Daphne W Bell, Daniel A Haber, and En Li. 1999. "DNA Methyltransferases Dnmt3a and Dnmt3b Are Essential for De Novo Methylation and Mammalian Development." *Cell* 99 (3): 247–257.

Olmsted, Frederick Law. 1860. *A Journey in the Back Country.* New York, NY: Mason Brothers.

Olsson, A. 2005. "The Role of Social Groups in the Persistence of Learned Fear." *Science* 309 (5735): 785–787.

Orfield, Gary, Genevieve Siegel-Hawley, and John Kucsera. 2012. *"E Pluribus" . . . Separation: Deepening Double Segregation for More Students.* Los Angeles, CA: The Civil Rights Project.

Oxford Dictionary. n.d. Retrieved from: https://en.oxforddictionaries.com/definition/racism.

Padgett, David A., and Ronald Glaser. 2003. "How Stress Influences the Immune Response." *Trends in Immunology* 24 (8): 444–448.

Padival, M.A., S.R. Blume, and J.A. Rosenkranz. 2013. "Repeated Restraint Stress Exerts Different Impact on Structure of Neurons in the Lateral and Basal Nuclei of the Amygdala." *Neuroscience* 246: 230–242.

Padival, Mallika, Danielle Quinette, and J Amiel Rosenkranz. 2013. "Effects of Repeated Stress on Excitatory Drive of Basal Amygdala Neurons in Vivo." *Neuropsychopharmacology* 38 (9): 1748–1762.

Palm, Wilhelm, and Titia de Lange. 2008. "How Shelterin Protects Mammalian Telomeres." *Annual Review of Genetics* 42 (1): 301–334.

Parks, C. G., D. B. Miller, E. C. McCanlies, R. M. Cawthon, M. E. Andrew, L. A. DeRoo, and D. P. Sandler. 2009. "Telomere Length, Current Perceived Stress, and Urinary Stress Hormones in Women." *Cancer Epidemiology Biomarkers and Prevention* 18 (2): 551–560.

Patton, George C., Carolyn Coffey, John B. Carlin, Craig A. Olsson, and Ruth Morley. 2004. "Prematurity at Birth and Adolescent Depressive Disorder." *British Journal of Psychiatry* 184 (05): 446–447.

Payne, B. Keith. 2001. "Prejudice and Perception: The Role of Automatic and Controlled Processes in Misperceiving a Weapon." *Journal of Personality and Social Psychology* 81 (2): 181–192. As cited by Chekroud, Adam M., Jim A. C. Everett, Holly Bridge, and Miles Hewstone. 2014. "A Review of Neuroimaging Studies of Race-Related Prejudice: Does Amygdala Response Reflect Threat?." *Frontiers in Human Neuroscience* 8.

Payne, B.Keith, Alan J Lambert, and Larry L Jacoby. 2002. "Best Laid Plans: Effects of Goals on Accessibility Bias and Cognitive Control in Race-Based Misperceptions of Weapons." *Journal of Experimental Social Psychology* 38 (4): 384–396.

Petit, B., B. Sykes, and B. Western. 2009. *Technical Report on Revised Population Estimates and NLSY79 Analysis Tables for the Pew Public Safety and Mobility Project.* Cambridge, MA: Harvard University.

Phelps, Elizabeth A., and Joseph E. LeDoux. 2005. "Contributions of the Amygdala to Emotion Processing: From Animal Models to Human Behavior." *Neuron* 48 (2): 175–187.

Phelps, Elizabeth A., and Laura A. Thomas. 2003. "Race, Behavior, and the Brain: The Role of Neuroimaging in Understanding Complex Social Behaviors." *Political Psychology* 24 (4): 747–758.

Phelps, Elizabeth A., Kevin J. O'Connor, William A. Cunningham, E. Sumie Funayama, J. Christopher Gatenby, John C. Gore, and Mahzarin R. Banaji. 2000. "Performance on Indirect Measures of Race Evaluation Predicts Amygdala Activation." *Journal of Cognitive Neuroscience* 12 (5): 729–738.

Phillips, D. I. W., D. J. P. Barker, C. H. D. Fall, J. R. Seckl, C. B. Whorwood, P. J. Wood, and B. R. Walker. 1998. "Elevated Plasma Cortisol Concentrations: A Link between Low Birth Weight and the Insulin Resistance Syndrome?." *The Journal of Clinical Endocrinology and Metabolism* 83 (3): 757–760.

Phillips, I. 2002. "Shared Governance on Black College Campuses." *Academe* 88 (4): 50–55.

Phillips, N., and S. Snyder. 2017. "Under Accreditation Threat, Cheyney to Hire Permanent President." *The Inquirer.* http://www.philly.com/philly/education/under-accredita-

tion-threat-cheyney-to-hire-permanent-president-20171109.
html.

Pleis, J.R., B.W. Ward, and J.W. Lucas. 2010. *Vital and Health Statistics: Summary Health Statistics for U.S. Adults: National Health Interview Survey, 2009*. Series 10: No. 249. Hyattsville, MD: U.S. Department of Health and Human Services, Centers for Disease Control and Prevention, National Center for Health Statistics.

Plotsky, Paul M., and Michael J. Meaney. 1993. "Early, Postnatal Experience Alters Hypothalamic Corticotropin-Releasing Factor (CRF) mRNA, Median Eminence CRF Content and Stress-Induced Release in Adult Rats." *Molecular Brain Research* 18 (3): 195–200.

Pradhan, Sriharsa, Albino Bacolla, Robert D. Wells, and Richard J. Roberts. 1999. "Recombinant Human DNA (Cytosine-5) Methyltransferase I Expression, Purification, and Comparison of De Novo and Maintenance Methylation" *Journal of Biological Chemistry* 274 (48), 33003- 33010.

Quirk, Gregory J, and Devin Mueller. 2007. "Neural Mechanisms of Extinction Learning and Retrieval." *Neuropsychopharmacology* 33 (1): 56–72.

Rajmohan, V., and E. Mohandas. 2007. "The Limbic System." *Indian Journal of Psychiatry* 49 (2): 132–139.

Ramos, K. 2010. "Remembering a Dark Page of History." *Valdosta Daily Times*.

Raven, P.H., G.B. Johnson, J.B. Losos, and S. Singer. 2005. *Biology*. 7th ed. New York: McGraw Hill.

Razin, A. 1998. "CpG Methylation, Chromatin Structure and Gene Silencing—a Three-Way Connection." *The EMBO Journal* 17 (17): 4905–4908.

Reardon, S. F. 2015. "School Segregation and Racial Academic Gaps." *Stanford Center for Education Policy Analysis*. http://cepa.stanford.edu/wp15-12.

Reece, J.B., N.A. Campbell, L.A. Urry, M.L. Cain, S.A. Wasserman, P.V. Minorsky, and R.A. Jackson. 2014. *Campbell Biology*. 9th ed. Boston: Benjamin Cummings/Pearson.

Reef, Joni, Sofia Diamantopoulou, Inge van Meurs, Frank C. Verhulst, and Jan van der Ende. 2011. "Developmental Trajectories of Child to Adolescent Externalizing Behavior and Adult DSM-IV Disorder: Results of a 24-Year Longitudinal Study." *Social Psychiatry and Psychiatric Epidemiology* 46 (12): 1233–1241.

Reeves, R., E. Rodrigue, and E. Kneebone. 2016. "Five Evils: Multidimensional Poverty and Race in America. *The Brookings Institution.* https://www.brookings.edu/wpcontent/uploads/2016/06/ReevesKneeboneRodrigue_MultidimensionalPoverty_FullPaper.pdf

Reik, Wolf, and Jörn Walter. 2001. "Evolution of Imprinting Mechanisms: The Battle of the Sexes Begins in the Zygote." *Nature Genetics* 27 (3): 255–256.

Richeson, Jennifer A., Andrew R. Todd, Sophie Trawalter, and Abigail A. Baird. 2008. "Eye-Gaze Direction Modulates Race-Related Amygdala Activity." *Group Processes and Intergroup Relations* 11 (2): 233–246.

Rinaldi, Arianna, Sara Vincenti, Francesca De Vito, Irene Bozzoni, Alberto Oliverio, Carlo Presutti, Paola Fragapane, and Andrea Mele. 2010. "Stress Induces Region Specific Alterations in MicroRNAs Expression in Mice." *Behavioural Brain Research* 208 (1): 265–269.

Robbins, S. and T.S. Jarmusz. 2017. "Shrouded in Secrecy." *The Daytona Beach News-Journal.*

Robinson, Monique, Andrew J. O. Whitehouse, John P. Newnham, Shelley Gorman, Peter Jacoby, Barbara J. Holt, and Michael Serralha et al. 2014. "Low Maternal Serum Vitamin D during Pregnancy and the Risk for Postpartum Depression Symptoms." *Archives of Women's Mental Health* 17 (3): 213–219.

Rodriguez-Bernal, Clara, Rebagliato, and Ballester. 2012. "Maternal Nutrition and Fetal Growth: The Role of Iron Status and Intake during Pregnancy." *Nutrition and Dietary Supplements*, 25.

Rosenkranz, J. Amiel, Emily R. Venheim, and Mallika Padival. 2010. "Chronic Stress Causes Amygdala Hyperexcitability in Rodents." *Biological Psychiatry* 67 (12): 1128–1136.

Rossiter, M. C. 1999. *Effects as Adaptations,* eds. T.A. Fox and C.W. Mousseau. London: Oxford University Press.

Roth, Tania L., Farah D. Lubin, Adam J. Funk, and J. David Sweatt. 2009. "Lasting Epigenetic Influence of Early-Life Adversity on the BDNF Gene." *Biological Psychiatry* 65 (9): 760–769.

Roth, Tania L., Eric D. Roth, and J. David Sweatt. 2010. "Epigenetic Regulation of Genes in Learning and Memory." *Essays in Biochemistry* 48: 263–274. doi:10.1042/bse0480263.

Roth, S.Y., J.M. Denu, and C.D. Allis. 2001. "Histone Acetyltransferases." *Annual Review of Biochemistry* 70: 81–120.

Rouse, C.E. 2007. "Quantifying the Costs of Inadequate Education: Consequences of the Labor Market. In *The Price We Pay: Economic and Social Consequences of Inadequate Education*, edited by C.R. Belfield and H.M. Levin, 99–124. Washington, DC: Brookings Institute Press.

Rubin, R. T., A. J. Mandell, and P. H. Crandall. 1966. "Corticosteroid Responses to Limbic Stimulation in Man: Localization of Stimulus Sites." *Science* 153 (3737): 767–768.

Rumberger, Russell W. 2011. *Dropping Out: Why Students Drop Out of High School and What Can Be Done about It*. Cambridge: Harvard University Press.

———. 2013. "Poverty and High School Dropouts. The Impact of Family and Community Poverty on High School Dropouts." *American Psychology Association.* http://www.apa.org/pi/ses/resources/indicator/2013/05/poverty-dropouts.aspx

Russell-Cole, Kathy, Midge Wilson, and Ronald E Hall. 1992. *The Color Complex: The Politics of Skin Color among African-Americans*. New York: Harcourt Brace Jovanovich Publishers.

SACSCOC, 2016, http://www.sacscoc.org. The college is still on warning as of June 23, 2017.

Santos, Andreia, Andreas Meyer-Lindenberg, and Christine Deruelle. 2010. "Absence of Racial, but Not Gender, Stereotyping in Williams Syndrome Children." *Current Biology* 20 (7): R307–R308.

Saphier, D., and S. Feldman. 1987. "Effects of Septal and Hippocampal Stimuli on Paraventricular Nucleus Neurons." *Neuroscience* 20 (3): 749–755.

Sapolsky, R. M., L. C. Krey, and B. S. McEwen. 1984. "Glucocorticoid-Sensitive Hippocampal Neurons Are Involved in Terminating the Adrenocortical Stress Response." *Proceedings of the National Academy of Sciences* 81 (19): 6174–6177.

Sato, Fumiaki, Soken Tsuchiya, Stephen J. Meltzer, and Kazuharu Shimizu. 2011. "MicroRNAs And Epigenetics." *FEBS Journal* 278 (10): 1598–1609.

Satyarthi, K. 2014. Education Is the Birthright of Every Child. https://www.careerindia.com/news/education-is-the-birth-right-every-child-kailash-satyarthi-012718.html

Schoeftner, Stefan, Aditya K Sengupta, Stefan Kubicek, Karl Mechtler, Laura Spahn, Haruhiko Koseki, Thomas Jenuwein, and Anton Wutz. 2006. "Recruitment of PRC1 Function at the Initiation of X Inactivation Independent of PRC2 and Silencing." *The EMBO Journal* 25 (13): 3110–3122.

Schumann, Cynthia Mills, and David G. Amaral. 2005. "Stereological Estimation of the Number of Neurons in the Human Amygdaloid Complex." *The Journal of Comparative Neurology* 491 (4): 320–329.

Schwartz, M., R. Skinner, and Z. Bowen. 2009. "Faculty, Governing Boards and Institutional Governance." *TIAA Institute.* https://www.tiaainstitute.org/sites/default/files/presenta-tions/2017-02/ahe_governance011003.pdf.

Shalev, Idan. 2012. "Early Life Stress and Telomere Length: Investigating the Connection and Possible Mechanisms." *Bioessays* 34 (11): 943–952.

Shammas, M.A. 2011. "Telomeres, Lifestyle, Cancer, and Aging." *Current Opinion in Clinical Nutrition and Metabolic Care,* 14 (1): 28–34.

Sheline, Yvette I., Mokhtar H. Gado, and Joseph L. Price. 1998. "Amygdala Core Nuclei Volumes Are Decreased in Recurrent Major Depression." *Neuroreport* 9 (9): 2023–2028.

Shonkoff, Jack P., and Deborah A Phillips. 2000. *From Neurons to Neighborhoods*. Washington: D.C: National Academic Press.

Shonkoff, J. P., A. S. Garner, B. S. Siegel, M. I. Dobbins, M. F. Earls, A. S. Garner, L. McGuinn, J. Pascoe, and D. L. Wood. 2012. "The Lifelong Effects of Early Childhood Adversity and Toxic Stress." *PEDIATRICS* 129 (1): e232–e246.

Siddiqui, S.V., U. Chatterjee, D. Kumar, A. Siddiqui, and N. Goyal. 2008. "Neuropsychology of Pre-Frontal Cortex." *Indian Journal of Psychiatry,* 50 (3): 202–208.

Siegle, Greg J., Roma O. Konecky, Michael E. Thase, and Cameron S. Carter. 2006. "Relationships between Amygdala Volume and Activity during Emotional Information Processing Tasks in Depressed and Never-Depressed Individuals." *Annals of the New York Academy of Sciences* 985 (1): 481–484.

"6-Year Graduation Rates at Many HBCUs Lower Than 20 Percent." 2018. *Atlanta Journal-Constitution*. https://www.ajc.com/news/local/year-graduation-rates-many-hbcus-lower-than-percent/TH1IXkSReeQEFQnnMjbxQN/new.html.

"Slavery in America." 2009. *History*. http://www.history.com/topics/black-history/slavery.

Smedley, Audrey. 1998. "Race and the Construction of Human Identity." *American Anthropologist* 100 (3): 690–702.

———. 1999. *Race in North America: Origin and Evolution of a Worldview*. 2nd ed. Boulder, CO: Westview Press.

Smedley, A., and B.D. Smedley. 2005. "Race as Biology Is Fiction; Racism as a Social Problem Is Real. Anthropological and Historical Perspectives on the Social Construction of Race." *American Psychologist,* 60 (1), 16–26.

Smith, M.K. 2015. "What Is Education? A Definition and Discussion." *The Encyclopaedia of Informal Education*. http://infed.org/mobi/what-is-education-a-definition-and-discussion.

Stanley, Damian, Elizabeth Phelps, and Mahzarin Banaji. 2008. "The Neural Basis of Implicit Attitudes." *Current Directions in Psychological Science* 17 (2): 164–170.

Stark, P.and Noel, A.M. 2015. Trends in High School Dropout and Completion Rates in United States: 1972–2012 (NCES 2015–

015). U.S. Department of Education. Washington: National Center for Education Statistics. Retrieved from: https://nces.ed.gov/pubs2015/2015015.pdf

Stephens, Brown, M. Christopher, J. John Harris III, and Jessica E. Stephens. 1999. "The Quest to Define Collegiate Desegregation: Black Colleges, Title VI Compliance, and Post-Adams Litigation." *The Journal of Negro Education* 68 (2): 238. doi:10.2307/2668129.

Steptoe, Andrew, Mark Hamer, Lee Butcher, Jue Lin, Lena Brydon, Mika Kivimäki, Michael Marmot, Elizabeth Blackburn, and Jorge D. Erusalimsky. 2011. "Educational Attainment but Not Measures of Current Socioeconomic Circumstances Are Associated with Leukocyte Telomere Length in Healthy Older Men and Women." *Brain, Behavior, and Immunity* 25 (7): 1292–1298.

Stern, Judith M. 1997. "Offspring-Induced Nurturance; Animal-Human Parallels." *Developmental Psychobiology* 31 (1): 19–37.

Stewart, W. 2013. "Is PISA flawed?." *Times Education Supplement Magazine.*

Stodghill, Ron. 2015. *Where Everybody Looks Like Me: At the Crossroads of America's Black Colleges and Culture.* New York, NY: HarperCollins Publishers.

Stuss, D.T., and R.T. Knight. 2002. "Past, Present and Future." In *Principles of Frontal Lobe Function*, edited by D.T. Stuss and R.T. Knight, 573–591. USA: Oxford University Press.

Sumner, William Graham. 1906. *Folkways A Study of the Sociological Importance of Usages, Manners, Customs, Mores, and Morals.* Boston, MA: Ginn and Company.

Surtees, Paul G., Nicholas W.J. Wainwright, Karen A. Pooley, Robert N. Luben, Kay-Tee Khaw, Douglas F. Easton, and Alison M. Dunning. 2012. "Educational Attainment and Mean Leukocyte Telomere Length in Women in the European Prospective Investigation into Cancer (EPIC)-Norfolk Population Study." *Brain, Behavior, and Immunity* 26 (3): 414–418.

Sykes, B. 2001. *The Seven Daughters of Eve.* New York, NY: W. W. Norton.

Tarry-Adkins, J. L., M. S. Martin-Gronert, J.-H. Chen, R. L. Cripps, and S. E. Ozanne. 2008. "Maternal Diet Influences DNA Damage, Aortic Telomere Length, Oxidative Stress, and Antioxidant Defense Capacity in Rats." *The FASEB Journal* 22 (6): 2037–2044.

Tatum, B.D. 1997. *"Why Are All Black Kids Siting Together in the Cafeteria?" And Other Conversation about Race.* New York, NY: Basic Books.

Taylor Jr., Q, n.d. U.S. History Timeline 1801–1900. http://www.quintardtaylor.com/us-history-timeline/ united-states-history-timeline-1801-1900.

Terbeck, S., G. Kahane, S. Metavish, J. Savulescu, P.J. Cowen, and M. Hewstone. 2012. "Propranolol Reduces Implicit Negative Racial Bias." *Psychopharmacology,* 222, 419–424.

The Atlanta Journal-Constitution; 2018. The 6-Year Graduation Rates at Many Hbcus Lower Than 20 Percent. Jan 29, 2018. Retrieved from: https://www.ajc.com/news/local/year-graduation-rates-ma-ny-hbcus-lower-than-percent/TH1IXkSReeQEFQnnMjbxQN/ new.html

"The Burning at Dyersburg: An NAACP Investigation." *The Crisis* 15, 178–183.

The Center for Measuring University Performance (MUP): The Top American Research Universities Annual Report for 2015. https://mup.asu.edu/sites/default/files/mup-2015-top-ameri-can-research-universities-annual-report.pdf

The Declaration of Independence; n.d. Retrieved from: http://www. ushistory.org/declaration/document/

Thomas, G. 2013. *Education: A Very Short Introduction.* Oxford: Oxford University Press.

Toldson, I.A. and G. Cooper. 2014. Historically Black Colleges and Universities Data Dashboard. US Department of Education, White House Initiative on Historically Black Colleges and Universities.

Tomiyama, A. Janet, Aoife O'Donovan, Jue Lin, Eli Puterman, Alanie Lazaro, Jessica Chan, and Firdaus S. Dhabhar et al. 2012. "Does Cellular Aging Relate to Patterns of Allostasis? An Examination of Basal and Stress Reactive HPA Axis and Telomere Length." *Physiology and Behavior* 106 (1): 40–45.

"Top Strategic Issues Facing HBCUs, Now and into the Future." 2014. *Association of Governing Boards.* https://www.agb.org/sites/default/files/legacy/2014TopStrategicIssuesFacingHB-CUs.pdf.

Toppo, G. 2016. "GAO Study: Segregation Worsening in US Schools." *USA Today.* https://www.usatoday.com/story/news/2016/05/17/gao-study-segregation-worsening-us-schools/845084381.

Trawalter, S., A.R. Todd, A.A. Baird, and J.A. Richeson. 2009. "Attending to Threat? : Race-Based Patterns of Selective Attention." *Journal of Experimental Social Psychology*, 44: 1322–1327.

Trelease, A.W. 1971. *White Terror: The Ku Klux Klan Conspiracy and Southern Reconstruction*, 3–5. As cited in *Lynching in America: Confronting the Legacy of Racial Terror*, n.d. https://lynchinginamerica.eji.org.

Tyrka, Audrey R., Lawrence H. Price, Hung-Teh Kao, Barbara Porton, Sarah A. Marsella, and Linda L. Carpenter. 2010. "Childhood Maltreatment and Telomere Shortening: Preliminary Support for an Effect of Early Stress on Cellular Aging." *Biological Psychiatry* 67 (6): 531–534.

Uchida, Shusaku, Akira Nishida, Kumiko Hara, Toshiki Kamemoto, Masatomo Suetsugi, Michiko Fujimoto, and Toshio Watanuki et al. 2008. "Characterization of the Vulnerability to Repeated Stress in Fischer 344 Rats: Possible Involvement of Microrna-Mediated Down-Regulation of the Glucocorticoid Receptor." *European Journal of Neuroscience* 27 (9): 2250–2261.

Umilta, C., F. Simion, and A. Valenza. 1996. "Newborn's Preference for Faces." *European Psychologist* 1 (3): 200–205. US Department of Education (1991). Retrieved from www2.ed.gov/about/offices/list/ocr/docs/hq9511.html

U.S. Department of Education; n.d., National Center for Education Statistics, Common Core of Data (CCD). "Public Elementary/Secondary School Universe Survey", 2012–13.

U.S. Department of Labor, Bureau of Labor Statistics (2013). http://www.bls.gov/cps/cpsaat07.htm.

U.S. News and World Report; 2018. Retrieved from: https://www.usnews.com/best-colleges/rankings/national-universities

Van de Kar, Louis D., and Martha L. Blair. 1999. "Forebrain Pathways Mediating Stress-Induced Hormone Secretion." *Frontiers in Neuroendocrinology* 20 (1): 1–48.

Vedantam, S. 2010. *The Hidden Brain: How Our Unconscious Minds Elect Presidents, Control Markets, Wage Wars, and Save Our Lives.* New York, NY: Spiegel & Grau.

Volk, Naama, Julius C. Pape, Mareen Engel, Anthony S. Zannas, Nadia Cattane, Annamaria Cattaneo, Elisabeth B. Binder, and Alon Chen. 2016. "Amygdalar MicroRNA-15A Is Essential for Coping with Chronic Stress." *Cell Reports* 17 (7): 1882–1891.

von Zglinicki, Thomas, Gabriele Saretzki, Wolf Döcke, and Christian Lotze. 1995. "Mild Hyperoxia Shortens Telomeres and Inhibits Proliferation of Fibroblasts: A Model for Senescence?." *Experimental Cell Research* 220 (1): 186–193.

von Zglinicki, Thomas. 2002. "Oxidative Stress Shortens Telomeres." *Trends in Biochemical Sciences* 27 (7): 339–344.

Waddington, C. H. 1942. "The Epigenotype." *Endeavor* 1: 18–20.

Wagner, Nancy O. n.d. "Slavery by Another Name." https://bento.cdn.pbs.org/hostedbento-prod/filer_public/SBAN/Images/Classrooms/Slavery%20by%20Another%20Name%20History%20Background_Final.pdf

Ward, Alan J. 1991. "Prenatal Stress and Childhood Psychopathology." *Child Psychiatry and Human Development* 22 (2): 97–110.

Warnock, M. 1986. "The Education of the Emotions." In *Education, Values and the Mind. Essays for R.S. Peters*, edited by D. Cooper, 182. London: Routledge and Keegan Paul.

Washington, B.T. 1895. Atlanta Exposition Speech. *Library of Congress' African American Odyssey.* http://historytools.davidjvoelker.com/sources/Washington-Atlanta.pdf.

Watt, D., and H. Roessingh. 1994. "Some You Win, Most You Lose: Tracking ESL Dropout in High School (1988–1993)." *English Quarterly,* 26, 5–7. As cited in Doll et al. 2013.

Weaver, Ian C.G., Nadia Cervoni, Frances A. Champagne, Ana C. D'Alessio, Shakti Sharma, Joanthan R. Seckl, Sergiy Demov, Moshe Szyf, and Micheal J. Meaney. 2004. "Epigenetic Programming by Maternal Behavior." *Nature Neuroscience* 7 (8): 847–854.

Weinhold, Bob. 2006. "Epigenetics: The Science of Change." *Environmental Health Perspectives* 114 (3): A160–A167.

Weinstock, M. 2001. "Alterations Induced by Gestational Stress in Brain Morphology and Behaviour of the Offspring." *Progress in Neurobiology* 65 (5): 427–451.

———. 2008. "The Long-Term Behavioural Consequences of Prenatal Stress." *Neuroscience and Biobehavioral Reviews* 32 (6): 1073–1086.

Wellman, David T. 1994. *Portraits of White Racism*. Cambridge: Cambridge Univ. Press.

Western, Bruce, and Becky Pettit. 2010. "Incarceration & Social Inequality." *Daedalus* 139 (3): 8–19.

Williams, W.J. 2006. "American Missionary Association." *Encyclopedia of North Carolina*. University of North Carolina Press. http://ncpedia.org.

Willms, J.D. 1999. "Quality and Inequality in Children's Literacy: The Effects Families, Schools and Communities." In *Developmental Health and Wealth of Nations: Social, Biological, and Educational Dynamics* edited by D. Keating and C. Hertzman, 72–94. New York: Guilford Press. As cited in Thomas, G. 2013. *Education: A Very Short Introduction*. Oxford, UK: Oxford University Press.

Wilson, Edward O. 2012. *The Social Conquest of Earth*. New York: NY: Liveright Publishing Corporation.

Woodson, C.G. 1933. *The Mis-Education of the Negro*. Washington, DC: Dover Education.

Wu, Guoyao, Beth Imhoff-Kunsch, and Amy Webb Girard. 2012. "Biological Mechanisms for Nutritional Regulation of Maternal Health and Fetal Development." *Paediatric and Perinatal Epidemiology* 26: 4–26.

Zeichner, S.L., P. Palumbo, Y. Feng, X. Xiao, D. Gee, J. Sleasman, M. Goodenow, R. Biggar, and D. Dimitrov. 1999. "Rapid Telomere Shortening in Children." *Blood* 93: 2824–2830.